River of Hope

A Journey of Faith, Hope, and Deliverance

Jeff Butler

Full Sail Publishing

RIVER OF HOPE

A Journey of Faith, Hope, and Deliverance

Copyright © 2024 by Jeff Butler

All rights reserved.

Published by Full Sail Publishing, Chicago, Illinois

Cover design by Jinx

No portion of this book may be reproduced in any form without written permission from the publisher or author except as permitted by U.S. copyright law.

For Crystal—my wife, best friend, and the love of my life.

Chapter One

The Well Runs Dry

The tiny shack, one of thousands crammed into the city dump, looked more like a forgotten heap of refuse than a home, pieced together from rusted metal panels on a dirt floor. Inside, the air was thick—too thick to breathe—stifling with human odor and oppressive heat. I stood in the doorway, the slice of sunlight behind me casting long shadows into the room. I couldn't see anything beyond the door's frame but knew what awaited me in the dark.

I came to Korah in Africa for this. To witness the suffering firsthand, to understand the depths of the people's struggles, and to bring whatever hope I could. I believed I could make a difference, however small, by being present. But now, in the doorway, my heart raced, and my feet felt cemented to the ground.

I couldn't step inside, not yet.

As my eyes adjusted, I saw people huddling together, writhing in the corners. Their bodies clumped and twisted, almost indistinguishable in the dim light from shadows. But their eyes—so many eyes—looked back at me. Pleading. Hopeless. Shining in the darkness.

Sweat slid down my back. My throat was dry as sandpaper. For a brief, disorienting moment, I flashed on the life I left behind: the sprawling green lawns and manicured gardens of my American home, the sparkling pool behind the house where my children played. The designer kitchen bursting with more food than my huge family needed.

It hit me like a punch in the gut: my arrogance, my privilege. How had I thought I could come to this hopeless place and make a difference?

One of my mission companions, Cindy, gasped, her hand flying to her mouth.

Another woman prayed softly, tears choking her voice. "Tend the sick, Lord Jesus; give rest to the weary, bless the dying, soothe the suffering, pity the afflicted..."

Bob, a stout man from San Antonio, took one step inside and backed up quickly. He stood next to the door, blocking precious light and casting deeper shadows into the room. The rest of the group hovered outside, shuffling uneasily.

Screams echoed deeper within the dump, cutting through the heavy silence. They came in waves, a haunting refrain that intertwined with the murmur of Amharic voices.

At least thirty lepers lived in the small room. Jammed together, their diseased and distorted faces regarded us calmly. Nearby, prosthetic arms and legs lay discarded in useless piles. Leprosy had taken noses, ears, lips, hands, and feet, leaving gaping holes and dangling, seeping wounds behind.

The lepers stared at us, and we stared back.

What are we supposed to do?

Stunned, despite previous trips to Africa, all my research, and everything we'd been told by our guides when they tried to prepare us for what we'd encounter at the infamous Korah dump leper city, I stood for what felt like an eternity, grappling with a flood of emotions, questions, and uncertainty.

The silence in the hut grew uncomfortably loud when the prayer fell silent.

I searched for sense in the terrible situation, for solutions to the many problems before me, but there were no solutions here. Only survival.

I had never felt so small, so utterly unprepared for the task at hand. Back home, I was the guy who got things done—a problem solver, a leader, a pastor, a husband, and a father. But here, where suffering ran so deep it was part of the landscape, I was useless.

My mind scrambled for a way out, some thread of hope I could cling to—but there was nothing. The enormity of it all drowned me. In Korah, I had nothing to give, stripped to my core and helpless in the face of such suffering.

"These poor people live their lives cut off from the world. Invisible to most, God sees them, and they are precious to Him. Help these souls, Lord, to see themselves as valuable too. I sense your presence among us today, God," the pastor leading us said, stepping forward, his hands outstretched, offering prayers and blessings to those who wanted them. One by one, he touched the lepers' faces while I stood frozen, paralyzed by the weight of it all.

What good were prayers in a place like this? What could a kind word do without doctors, medicine, or food? And yet, as I looked at the pastor, I saw a sense of peace in the eyes of those he prayed for. Even in this place, a prayer could bring a glimmer of hope, a reminder that they were not entirely forgotten.

We regrouped outside.

The streets of Korah were a maze of filth and misery. Everywhere I looked, people clung to life by the thinnest of threads. Children with hollow eyes and dirt-streaked faces ran barefoot through the trash-strewn paths, foraging for scraps. Elderly men and women, their bodies twisted and ravaged by leprosy and disease, shuffled along, limbs half-missing, eyes distant and hollow.

The heat rose in waves from the garbage-strewn ground. A few feet away, a dead dog lay bloated, legs stiff and pointed toward the sky. A small child, barely clothed in rags, sat nearby, wailing with hunger. Belly distended, she clutched a scrap of garbage to her chest like a treasure.

I had no idea how to help. *Why did I bring other people to this terrible place?*

***

This was not my first journey to Africa. Yet, this time felt different, more profound, and urgent, as if each step carried the weight of my mission. I came here with conviction, believing my role as a leader and pastor could inspire genuine change. My ambition was strong, rooted in the faith that meaningful work could be achieved through unity and compassion. I wasn't alone; I brought fifteen passionate souls from my congregation, all eager to serve.

Abebe Getachew, a trusted Ethiopian guide and cherished friend, led us to the places closest to his heart, the homes for widows and orphans he helped build, and finally, to Korah, the infamous leper city.

I thought I was ready for it. I thought I knew what to expect. But Korah was like nothing I'd ever seen before.

"Korah doesn't exist officially," Abebe had explained earlier that day when we neared the settlement. "The name means cursed. It was founded long ago to house lepers near a hospital. Now, over 150,000 people live here—outcasts, the poorest of the poor. They survive by scavenging from the city dump. The children compete with adults for food and scraps."

"Why doesn't the city do something about it?" Cindy from Grapevine asked. She had kind blue eyes and wore a jaunty pink scarf around her head.

"In exchange for being allowed to live in Korah, the government ignores them completely, as if they don't exist, like tossed-out garbage," I said, looking forward to seeing another side of poverty, a place where some of the orphans I'd met on previous trips came from. I thought that if we could help families in Korah, we could prevent more orphans.

"How can the government ignore an entire community of so many poor and sick people?" Cindy frowned.

"It is easy to ignore what you cannot see." Abebe's expressive, dark eyes flickered with emotion and purpose as he spoke of Korah; he wanted me to see it, to understand its story. His passion for the people living in the dumped city convinced me to add it to our itinerary. But listening to him before we arrived in Korah made me think about how deeply my previous trips to Africa affected me. I worried for myself and the people I'd convinced to come with me this time.

"Conditions, as you can imagine, are abysmal in this place, entirely shut off from the normal world. Only the poorest and most desperate people live there, so it is truly shocking to see the thousands upon thousands with no other choice, nowhere to go, no one to help them." Abebe's voice held the sadness we all felt, though he spoke matter-of-factly, the way only someone who has worked in such terrible places for many years can. "The people you meet today are the poorest in the world. They have been abandoned, rejected, outcast, and discarded. Aid, what little there is, does not reach people considered utterly hopeless by most organizations. That is why you being here today matters so much."

As they heard about leprosy and horrors the likes of which they'd probably never imagined, concerned glances passed between several people in my group. Everyone wore newly nervous expressions. Orphans were one thing. Lepers, another.

"What happens if I touch a leper? Can you catch it? Isn't it contagious?" one of the most nervous men, Bob, asked.

"I didn't know leprosy still existed," a woman with worried eyes said. "Wasn't that a disease back in Bible times?"

Abebe reassured us as much as possible from the front of the bus while still trying to prepare our group for the shocking things we'd see in Korah and how it would make us feel. "You need not worry. It takes months of close contact to catch leprosy from another. We'll be fine."

I don't think this alleviated anyone's concerns. Still, everyone seemed to relax when we turned our attention to the poor people we'd meet dropping off supplies to this community so desperately needing help.

"What do they usually do for food?" Cindy asked.

"The lepers send their children to the dump daily to forage second-hand food. Food that has already been used and then thrown in the trash," Abebe explained.

Surprisingly, the children of the lepers seemed mostly immune to leprosy. Still, they faced daily dangers in the city dump, victims of abuse, rape, severe injuries, and infections made worse by lack of medical care. I spared the group these details.

"The dump is high, like a mountain range. Like compost, the piles get hot. In many places, the trash burns. The children sometimes fall into these fires, get severely burned, and even die." Abebe shook his head but did not elaborate further.

I pictured hell on earth and a disease that destroys and disfigures everything, like a monster that steals a person's sense of value and dignity along with their limbs. I imagined precious and innocent children on the very edge of despair and death. Looking around the bus carrying us to the dump city, I saw the vivid descriptions of life in Korah had battered our group badly. Still, nothing could have prepared us for what we saw that day.

We stopped first near the outskirts of Korah, by a small church in a squat building that looked like the others on the street, to meet the mission's pastor, Pastor Nunesh. A slight man with sunken cheeks and a warm smile, he grew up in Korah and stayed, called to serve his people there.

"He does what he can," Abebe said. "With very little help from anyone else, he strives to make a difference in the lives of the people of Korah and brings much relief with his kindness and leading others here."

Pastor Nunesh told us encouraging stories about people the mission helped to balance some of the horrors we'd see before we set off on foot down narrow, twisting mud paths between corrugated tin shacks.

Everything around us changed within a few hundred feet, like walking into another world, a place of nightmares. As we walked through the narrow alleys of Korah, tin shacks rose around us in the mountains of garbage. The air reeked with the stench of waste and rot. Children ran barefoot through the refuse, their faces dirty, their clothes torn. Everywhere, there were reminders of the sickness that permeated this place—leprosy, HIV, tuberculosis. The enormity of it all crushed my heart.

We moved at a crawl to avoid stepping in open ditches that served as sewers or walking on dead, rotting animals or people who sat in the dirt watching us pass blankly.

Wires ran overhead and at eye level, crisscrossing the alley and giving some families bootlegged basic electricity.

"Watch the sharp metal edges of the buildings and roofs! They will deliver a major gash to your head," Abebe warned. "Also, watch for downed wires and avoid stepping in the puddles. That is urine."

We turned a corner and came face to face with a group of lepers, just as described—disfigured faces and limbs, their clothes sparse and worn. The sight hit us hard. The people in my group shifted uncomfortably, visibly unsure of what to do, frozen in place as the pastor introduced us.

Unlike the other Ethiopians we met at our hotel in Addis Ababa, who welcomed us warmly, the lepers kept their distance, their restraint noticeable.

"Nobody ever touches them," Pastor Nunesh said softly. "They are outcasts."

Chuck, a burly former Marine from Ft. Worth, broke the tension. "Do you think they'd mind a hug?" he asked, his voice breaking. Without waiting for a reply, he stepped forward, arms wide open, and one of the lepers embraced him tightly. His act of kindness shattered the invisible wall between us. Inspired by his courage, several of us followed Chuck's lead, offering our own hugs.

I embraced a frail man who felt almost weightless in my arms. His skin was dry and fragile, his arms like delicate twigs. At that moment, it felt like I wasn't just hugging him but receiving a hug from something far greater, something divine. Emotions welled up, crashing over me.

The lepers' smiles radiated an unfamiliar joy and love, something I struggled to understand. In their smiles, I found a glimmer of hope—a reminder of the profound value of human connection, even amidst the deepest suffering. How could they find happiness when they were shunned by the world, labeled as unclean and unwanted? What would that do to my own sense of self-worth? If I were that ill, with nothing but the compassion of a few strangers offering me nothing but prayers and hugs, could I still greet the world with such love and joy?

Before I finished processing the moment and my new questions, we moved on, delivering sacks of teff grain to the homes of several lepers. The dwellings and people were all unbelievably poor, but the house with the many lepers crammed together in darkness attacked my senses. The smell of sour body odor and urine hung thick in the air long after we walked away, shaken to our cores by what we'd seen and our inability to truly help.

As we made our way deeper into the colony, delivering scant supplies, we met many families, each one more heart-wrenching than the last. But it was a young mother holding her infant child who would haunt me forever.

We walked into another forgotten shack and found a teenage girl around fifteen, wearing rags, holding a tiny baby. Her eyes met mine, her gaunt face streaked with tears, a baby cradled in her arms, its tiny body limp. The room around us felt too small, too dark, like the walls were closing in, pressing me against the suffocating weight of her need. She didn't speak. She didn't have to. Her hollow stare, quivering lips, and the fragile hope that I might have something—anything—to offer her said it all. *What are you going to do for me?*

I felt rooted to the dirt floor, my throat tight and dry, my chest heavy with the crushing weight of hopelessness. I had come here to help—to bring hope, to lead others in this mission of mercy—but standing in that shack, I had nothing. No answers. No quick solutions. Not even a word of comfort.

Her child let out a soft whimper, barely audible, its tiny body pressed against its mother in desperation, and I had to fight the urge to look away, to run, to retreat from the pain that radiated from them.

"We have to move on," the pastor said from the doorway, his voice low but insistent.

I nodded, though every fiber of my being screamed to stay—to fix this, somehow, to make it better. But what could I do? I had nothing for her. No food to sustain her beyond a few days, no medicine to cure all her ails, and no answers that would lift her out of the hell she lived in. What good were we, walking through this slum and dropping off supplies that would be gone in days? What difference could we make in a place like this?

Guilt and helplessness crushed me as I stepped back into the harsh sunlight, the young mother's face burned into my mind. I had walked away from her just as I walked away from so many others that day. The weight of my own inadequacy settled over me like a shroud. I took a step backward, then another, the light from the doorway swallowing me up as I left the young mother and her child behind, their silent plea echoing in my mind. *What are you going to do for me?*

I asked myself again why I came to Ethiopia, to this desperate place. But as I struggled with my sense of failure, a new determination grew within me—a commitment to make a more significant impact in the future, to not let this helplessness be the end of my story here.

The members of our group huddled close together as we moved deeper into the slum, each one of us lost in our own thoughts, shaken by the scenes unfolding before us. Every step felt heavier than the last, my chest tight with a gnawing sense of guilt.

Abebe's words rang in my ears. He had tried to prepare us, warning us about what we would see in Korah—the lepers, the children scavenging in the trash, the people left behind by the world. But hearing it and seeing it were two entirely different things.

"This is life here," Abebe told us. "This is survival."

But it didn't feel like life. It felt like death. Slow, unrelenting death.

I thought I was ready. I thought we could offer something—hope, dignity, relief—by coming here. But standing there, surrounded by the sick, the starving, the forgotten, I had no answers. No solutions. I was drowning.

As the day wore on, the faces of the people we met blurred together—each one a reflection of the same desperate plea. Children with distended bellies and bare feet. Mothers clutching babies too weak to cry. Lepers whose bodies were slowly being consumed by disease. Every face a mirror of suffering, of hopelessness.

When we returned to the bus, an oppressive weight settled over me, heavier than the sweltering heat. The others murmured quietly, trying to make sense of what we'd witnessed, but I couldn't join them. What could I say? We had come to help, but as I climbed onto the bus, the truth gnawed at me: what help had we really given?

The bus rattled over uneven roads, but the images of Korah refused to fade. The young mother, her baby too weak to cry, her face etched with despair. The rotting dog sprawled in the trash, stiff and bloated under the relentless sun. The stench of decay and death seemed to seep into my skin, sticking to me as if I could never wash it away.

What are you going to do for me? The woman's eyes—pleading, empty—haunted me as though they stared through the glass of the bus window, asking the one question I couldn't answer.

I had come to lead, to serve, to offer hope. But what difference had we made in that place where suffering stretched endlessly? I had convinced others we could make an impact, but when I'd stood in the heart of Korah, surrounded by sickness, hunger, and hopelessness, I had been stripped of the certainty I brought with me.

The bus jolted. I gripped the seat in front of me. The murmurs of the mission team barely registered. Outside, the city's outskirts began to replace the slums, but inside, I was still trapped. Trapped in that dark room with the young mother and her dying child. Trapped by the suffocating guilt of realizing I had nothing to give her—no solutions, no answers.

The bus rumbled on, the sun sinking lower in the sky, casting long shadows across the landscape. But my mind wasn't in Korah anymore. It had drifted back to my first trip to Africa, years before, when I arrived just as wide-eyed, just as hopeful. I wasn't ready then, either.

That first trip had been humbling. I came eager to serve, full of dreams and naive expectations, only to be confronted with a reality I wasn't prepared for. It shook me but also cracked something open in me. I saw overwhelming suffering, but I glimpsed something deeper. Something that stayed with me long after I'd returned home.

But this...this was different.

Korah wasn't just humbling. It was crushing. The weight of it pressed down on me, suffocating, with no hope in sight. This time, there were no moments of grace, no glimpses of joy. Only despair. The young mother's hollow eyes kept pulling me back, her question lingering: *What are you going to do for me?*

Addis Ababa's vibrant streets bustled with life just miles away from Korah's devastation. How close these two worlds existed, yet how distant they felt. I stared out the window, feeling the weight of the past and present bearing down on me. That first trip to Africa had been the beginning of something—though I hadn't known it then. It set me on this path, a journey that brought me here to this moment, where I felt more lost than ever.

But if that first trip had taught me anything, it was that sometimes, being lost is where you find what truly matters. It showed me that amid overwhelming uncertainty and despair, there are moments that can shape us, moments where even the smallest acts of love and compassion can create ripples of hope.

Another memory came rushing in from my first trip to this continent, a trip that forever changed my life trajectory. A time when I found hope and something I didn't know I searched for—the children. Their faces rose in my mind like ghosts from the past—wide eyes, shy smiles, hands reaching out, not for food or supplies, but for something more lasting. For love. For a family.

I came to Africa to make a difference. To help. To be part of something bigger than myself. But as the sun set in that desolate place, I could only see my failure staring back at me.

What are you going to do for me?

I didn't have an answer. And that was the most terrifying part of all.

Chapter Two

Clinging to Shore

The first time I visited Ethiopia, I stayed at a Catholic guest house in the capital city of Addis Ababa. My small room was simple and clean, with a hard mattress and a pillow like a brick.

I woke after a few hours of sleep, completely disoriented in this strange new place after my nearly thirty-hour journey, to a strange, steady noise in the distance—eerie, wailing music and chanting. I couldn't make out words, but the songs made me sad and lonely.

Everything outside my tiny window was stunningly different from any place I'd traveled before, with many strange new sights, smells, and sounds. Tucked into the foothills of mountains, the town featured a skyline stuffed with skyscrapers, but contrasts between development and destruction, old worlds and new, were everywhere I looked.

"Ethiopia has never been colonized," my friend, Ben, told me when we first discussed his mission work in Africa. "Which means it's more backward than you might expect. But it is a place of contrasts. Of extreme wealth and poverty. The things we're able to do there for orphans are incredible. You should come with me sometime. Someone like you could make a real difference there."

Ben and I worked together in medical sales, and he knew me well enough to know I was the proud father of several adopted kids and a pastor at my local church. I enjoyed hearing about his mission organization's work with orphans and the needy in Africa, but I wasn't interested in going to Ethiopia.

When I told my wife Crystal about Ben's invitation, I figured she would be my out. We'd just adopted another baby, adding to our already large family. There was no way Chris would let me go to Africa right now. The timing was terrible.

"Ben invited me to go on a mission trip to Ethiopia with the organization he serves to see what they're doing for orphans there," I told her one night as she folded laundry.

"What did you say?" she asked, her tone unreadable.

"I told him I would pray about it," I said, helping her with a fitted sheet printed with cartoon race cars. "But I don't want to go," I added quickly.

"Why not?"

"I have my hands full at work, and I'm up to my elbows in ministry activities of my own. We just adopted a baby. The timing is terrible. I can't leave you alone to manage the house and our kids. Why not? I'm sure I can think of more reasons why not if those aren't enough." I grinned.

She laughed, handing me a bunch of pillowcases to fold. "I think you should go. How often do people get a chance to go to Africa?"

Though we'd been married many years by then, and Chris still surprised me sometimes, I hadn't expected this. "You think I should go? To Africa? They have cannibals there! Diseases. I'd be gone weeks."

"Have you forgotten your promise to be open to what God brings our way? This seems like one of those times to me." She smirked.

I frowned but nodded in agreement, remembering when we agreed to let God bring us what He would when we'd struggled with infertility years earlier, and I had trouble understanding why He seemed to forsake us. "Yeah, but surely God didn't mean I should go to Africa just because Ben asked me."

Chris shrugged, walking away to put up the clean laundry, but my mind whirled with the possibilities. As she disappeared down the hall, I stood there, the house's quiet settled around me. Could it really be that simple? Was this a test of faith, or was I trying to force meaning where there was none? My mind wrestled with the questions, caught between doubt and a strange pull I couldn't quite name. The thought of Africa, of Ben's invitation, suddenly felt heavier—like something far bigger than the two of us.

I'm going!

***

Ethiopia proved to be a land of ancient wonders and modern marvels. History whispered to me from every stone. The past and present seemed intertwined, creating a tapestry of culture and resilience. I couldn't shake the feeling that I stepped into something far bigger than I had ever imagined.

As different as everything was, at first, it felt like any other trip I'd experienced: getting to know a new culture, taking in the sights, learning the place's history, eating local food, and seeing the sights.

In the 13th century, I learned, the Solomonic Dynasty ruled Ethiopia, claiming descent from the biblical King Solomon. They ruled for centuries, leaving an indelible mark on the country's culture and history. Looking at pictures on the internet before my trip, immersing myself in the rich history, I could almost feel the presence of these emperors in the ancient churches of Lalibela, carved out of solid rock, or as I looked with awe at the towering obelisks of Axum, testaments to the power and grandeur of the Solomonic Dynasty. In person, they were even more spectacular.

Things took a sad turn in the mid-20th century. In 1974, a military coup overthrew Emperor Haile Selassie, ushering in the Derg regime, a socialist military government. The Dergs ruled through political repression, civil war, and economic hardship.

"You can almost hear the echoes of gunfire and the cries of the oppressed as you walk through some parts of Addis Ababa. You can see the scars of conflict in the faces of the people and the ruins of buildings that once stood tall," Ben said in the days leading up to our trip. "The Derg regime was a dark chapter in Ethiopia's history, but it also sparked a yearning for freedom and democracy that grows only stronger. Today is a time of hope and renewal. Being part of that is amazing! There's just so much to do."

After the Derg regime collapsed, Ethiopia transitioned to a multi-party democracy. Since then, the country has faced new challenges, including ethnic conflicts, poverty, and food security concerns. It was hard to imagine the kind of poverty Ben described.

"Despite all this, the people of Ethiopia are determined to build a brighter future. You will meet some of them during our trip and see for yourself," Ben said.

I couldn't wait to get out and see the work Ben told me so much about in the weeks leading up to our trip. I was eager to visit the orphanages and see how the mission helped children there. I sell medical supplies for a living, and as much as what we provide helps people, I was excited to have a more direct impact on the lives of children in need. As the father of several adopted children, my heart was especially touched by the plight of the many orphans in Ethiopia. As a pastor, I taught empathy and the charity of Jesus. Now, I had a real chance to practice what I preached in a place where people needed help the most.

Before seeing what breakfast was like in Ethiopia, I prayed alone in my little room. "Lord, open my eyes today to help me see the people of Ethiopia as your servant. Amen."

In the dining hall, strange smells of unfamiliar food welcomed me. Several mission team members greeted me warmly and invited me to grab a plate and eat. I reviewed the food options, which mainly consisted of stews of various sorts served alongside a spongy pancake-like bread called injera with a tangy flavor similar to sourdough. To eat the stews, you tear off a small piece of injera and use it to scoop up the food. The sponginess of the bread soaks up the heavily spiced sauces of the stews. That first day, I bypassed that because of a weak stomach that doesn't do well with new things. I was relieved to find scrambled eggs and plain bread. The best part was the unique, robust coffee. Ethiopia is the birthplace of coffee and since coffee is one of the greatest joys in life as far as I am concerned, things were off to a good start.

I enjoyed our first breakfast gathering, chatting with the other mission team members excitedly about what we would experience that day.

Abebe, the mission's in-country director, arrived as we finished breakfast. I met him briefly the night before when he met our team at the airport and drove us to the guesthouse. A delightful man with a contagious smile and laughter, he wore a well-trimmed beard, tidy glasses, and a baseball cap. He radiated a gentle, humble spirit, dressed professionally in a nice sports coat and slacks.

"Please, meet my wife, Abonesh. She serves in the mission also." Abebe's eyes glowed with pride as he looked at her.

Tall and incredibly beautiful, Abonesh's poise and gentle demeanor struck me immediately. She had an uncommon elegance and grace. Like her husband, she wore Western, professional clothing and sneakers and glowed with good nature.

After the introductions, the couple hugged us like long-lost friends, greeting each mission team member deliberately and without any rush.

"Ethiopians love long hugs and will warmly welcome you every time, wanting to learn everything about you," Ben said. "You get used to it!"

Showered with kindness and care wherever I went, I was in good shape if this indicated what my trip would be like, I thought.

"What was the music and chanting I heard this morning?" I asked Abebe as we left the hotel in a large van he'd packed with things he'd leave behind at the places we visited.

"You must have heard the Orthodox Church's call to morning prayer." He smiled widely, pulling into a busy street as I looked for a seatbelt. "It is a beautiful way to wake, yes?"

My first close-up look at Ethiopia's capital city overloaded my senses. What struck me most was the overwhelming number of people everywhere—streams of people walked next to buildings and in the streets as cars zipped around them in every direction, horns honking. There seemed to be no traffic lights or signs. It was every driver for themselves. Even downtown rush hour back home was no match for this.

The acrid stench of diesel fumes filled my nostrils as our van moved slowly through the congested streets. Windows down, foreign smells, sights, and sounds flooded my senses, exhilarating me.

As we traveled through the bustling streets, I saw the signs of progress Ben mentioned—new buildings rising under cranes, businesses thriving, and young people eager to make their mark on the world. The place was captivating, a city that blended ancient traditions with the vibrant energy of a modern metropolis. Nestled amidst the stunning highlands, Addis Ababa means a new flower in Amharic, and

I could see why. It's a city blooming with cultural diversity, historical significance, and a unique charm that left me breathless.

As we explored the city further, we saw the Holy Trinity Cathedral, a masterpiece of Ethiopian Orthodox architecture, and the National Museum of Ethiopia.

The bustling Merkato, Africa's largest open-air market, was a sensory overload of sights, sounds, and aromas we only drove past that day. Though I had no interest in haggling over souvenirs, I reminded myself not to forget to get some things to bring home to the family.

"Very close is the serenity of the Entoto Mountains, where you can visit the Maryam Church, one of the oldest churches in Ethiopia, and enjoy panoramic views of the city, but I do not think we will have time for that this trip," Abebe said with regret in his voice.

"I'm amazed at the contrasts and how different it is from what I expected, how cosmopolitan even." It disturbed me to know that in this land that seemed so vibrant and filled with possibilities, so many people lived without the necessities for survival, and so many children suffered as orphans.

"It is stunning at night—a tapestry of twinkling lights, Art Deco architecture, traditional restaurants, lively cultural entertainment, and cafes," Abebe said with pride.

"It defies expectations." I'd never been to a place where ancient traditions coexisted so much with the pulse of modernity. The city captivated my senses and challenged my preconceptions.

"Ethiopia is a land where ancient traditions mesh with modern ambitions. It is a land of resilience and hope, where the past and present collide to create a unique and captivating story that I wish more people knew," Abebe said. "That said, we have far to go, many to help, as you will see."

Our van had to stop and go several times. The traffic snarled, thick around us in whatever lanes people could find. The city revealed itself in bits and pieces, each stranger than the last.

"What's with the scales everywhere?" I asked, noticing scales on corners and outside entrances to small shops, where people lined up to weigh themselves. "Why's everyone weighing themselves today?"

Abebe grinned. "Here, the fatter you are, the richer you are, the more blessed."

"So, they're checking to see if they are more or less blessed today?" I laughed at the foreign concept, trying to imagine the same thing in America, where many seem diet-obsessed.

"Indeed. Rich people here are all fat, so fat is a good thing. Most are not so lucky as you will see today also."

We stopped for a man driving a small flock of sheep across the road. A woman standing on a corner locked eyes with me and moved toward our van. She raised her hand, palm up. Wearing a baby on her hip and ragged tatters for clothing, she was malnourished and desperate for help. Her eyes expressed nothing but despair.

I couldn't look away from her, never more aware of my wealth and success, my belly full of breakfast, and laughter dying on my lips.

She moved closer. Eyes full of need and pain, she said something I did not understand and reached for my arm.

Abebe's voice broke through the spell the woman put on me as I sat transfixed, looking into her eyes. "Close your window," he said, rolling his up quickly. "They like to grab what they can."

"That baby was so small. She didn't have any shoes. I, I..." I struggled to describe what I'd seen and how it made me feel. I imagined Chris at home with our new baby, fresh from a bath, health and happiness shining in her eyes, and my stomach twisted with despair.

"It is sad, but it is best not to give any money to the street beggars," Abebe said.

We moved slowly forward. As we passed, the woman's eyes dropped, and her shoulders sagged as hope faded.

"But I could've helped her."

"I do not wish to sound immune to their suffering, but there are thousands like her, and poverty is everywhere you look," Abebe said. "We focus where we can do the most good."

I nodded, unprepared for my rush of emotions and helplessness. As we traveled farther from the more modern side of town where the hotel was, I saw he was right. Poverty, which only grew worse as we drove on, was everywhere.

Already overwhelmed and not even halfway through my first day in Africa, I was close to destitute people in need, yet still so far away, driving past them like a tourist at a safari park.

Remembering my morning prayer, I tried to take it all in, to see without judgment of anyone, including myself.

We passed an endless lineup of mostly makeshift housing made of scrap wood and corrugated tin sheeting, exposed bootleg electric wires zig-zagging overhead to the lucky ones. As in the other parts of town, people flooded the streets and alleys, but many wore rags and had bare feet and hollow cheeks.

Cooking happened outside the tiny shacks. Smoke and strange smells filled the air. Fires burned here and there, though I saw few people eating.

"Do families all live together?" I asked, noticing how many of the tiny homes were connected.

"It is best to stick together here. Community is all some have," Abebe said.

Children sat with their mothers and older relatives outside, kept close. Most were very thin and poor, with rounded bellies and tiny legs, but they smiled, laughed, and shouted back and forth like kids anywhere.

Many women carried large plastic containers on their heads, trekking long distances to fetch scarce water that required boiling to make it remotely safe.

"They do this several times a day for the whole family." Abebe nodded at a group of women we passed, who laughed together amid their dire circumstances. "Here, the saying, 'It takes a village,' is true. When you have nothing, you help each other. It's the only way to survive."

I thought of all the families I knew who hardly spent time together in their big houses and busy lives, all the nannies, daycares, caregivers, teachers, and layers between parents, their kids, and people. Many of us don't know our neighbors, let alone hang out with them or care for them.

"They're better at community than we are. In some ways, people here seem closer, more connected, than back home," I said, surprised and humbled at assumptions I'd made without knowing about the people here and how they lived.

We arrived at the first orphanage after a long, bumpy ride.

"This is a widows' and orphans' home, one of only a few like it," Abebe said. "Elderly widows with no place to go look after orphans and older children help the widows as much as possible. There is much love shared by all. The mission does amazing things here with precious little resources. You will see!"

It was beautiful, the older women holding orphan babies and the children helping the elderly widows who needed it, everyone working together to care for one another.

"I've never seen anything like it. What a great idea!" My heart was touched. This was what I had come to see.

Abebe smiled. "The executive director of the orphanage had the vision to start such a home, to care for widows and orphans together and help them all at the same time."

It was truly remarkable. Though sparse, the place was clean and tidy, and the widows and orphans looked happy and clean.

"The orphans give the widows a sense of purpose and fulfillment as they once again can love on babies in their later years of life," Abebe said as we unloaded the van and brought supplies into a small storeroom.

"Many widows who live outside the orphanage in the surrounding community come to receive supplies," Ben said.

We carried in several massive bags of teff (an Ethiopian grain-like staple) and other food supplies, watching as one person after another came to get their share. Seeing a small older woman heave a large bag of teff on her back was rewarding. Here was one person who would not go hungry for a while. I started to feel better, eager to learn more about the mission's work at the widows' and orphans' home and how I could help.

"Let me help," I said to a frail woman hunched over from years of heavy burdens.

Abebe translated, extending my offer to carry the woman's heavy load.

They exchanged a few words, and he smiled as she walked away. "She declined, saying to me the burden of hunger is far heavier than the burden of this teff. She goes in gratitude, bidding you to help others more in need."

I had never felt the burden of hunger and couldn't relate to carrying such a thing alone. For the first time, someone humbled me that I wanted to help. This would be a recurring theme of my early visits to Ethiopia.

We spent the rest of the day visiting other orphanages and playing with the children we met. There was a story of loss for every child, and there were so many children. Like all children, these played, laughed, and ran. Some were loud and boisterous, while others were shy, reserved, or withdrawn. Everyone was curious about us and why we were there. Some seemed highly nervous, avoiding our eyes and staying safely behind the widows.

"They have seen this many times before. Many are too little to understand why they are at the orphanage and why some friends leave and never return. How can the little ones understand the concept of adoption? Where did their friends go? Would they have to leave someday? Would these kind but odd-looking white people take them away, too? It is too much for most to try and understand at such an early age," Abebe explained. "But we do our best to let them know you are friends who bring hope and goodness with you."

"I see," I said, though I did not. So many children had lost their families for one reason or another. It was hard to process. "Some of the children are quite a bit older. Have they lived here all their lives?" The thought made my stomach churn.

"Many have lived at the orphanage for several years, longing for adoption before they age out at sixteen and must leave the orphanage. With no family to help or support them, most end in tragedy left to fend for themselves on the streets alone," Abebe said.

This news hurt my heart. These were no longer the children I'd heard about in some distant African country in extreme poverty or watched on TV as a sad song played. These were actual children in front of me, grabbing my hand, wanting to sit on my lap and be held and hugged like all children do. Like my kids do.

The contrast between their lives and mine hit me hard, though I thought I'd been prepared. How could God have made these children so poor, helpless, and vulnerable while deciding I would be wealthy and successful enough to provide for my family comfortably and effortlessly? I struggled to make sense of a world where so many children needed parents, food, and homes, where even the most basic needs were impossible to meet, in contrast to the abundance of America, where most of us have so much more than we realize. I could not reconcile the imbalance or understand God's reasoning for allowing so much suffering.

As we played with the kids throughout the afternoon, the heaviness of the situation lifted for a bit. My thoughts turned to lighter things as I forced myself to be in the moment and enjoy my time with the children. For a while, I pretended the massive problems I'd learned about here didn't exist, focusing on two kids, both five years old—a cute little boy named Joshua and Aliyah, a timid girl.

Even before Abebe introduced us, Joshua caught my eye, leading blind widows around, acting as their eyes. An extremely cheerful boy, he smiled constantly, moved fast, and wore shabby oversized clothes. Full of energy, he proved exceptionally good at soccer when we kicked the ball together in the small, dirt courtyard of the orphanage.

Abebe called Joshua over after our group had been there for a while and sorted through the boxes and packages we'd brought. He presented a brand-new set of western-style clothes donated through the organization to the shy boy, whose face lit up with joy at the prospect of receiving them.

Joshua couldn't stop smiling as he marched around in the crisp, new jeans and a T-shirt with Elmo on it, showing everyone his new outfit. The clothes meant more to him than any I'd ever owned, and it warmed my heart to see the boy's happiness and pride. I thought of my closet back home, full of expensive suits and ties, shoes in every color and type, workout clothes, and just hanging around the house clothes, and vowed to donate some.

I smiled, watching Abebe wipe away a tear. "Abebe, you have such a tender heart for all the children," I said.

"Maybe because I was orphaned too, cast away by my own family. Though I like to think I would be kind anyway," Abebe said.

"What happened to you?"

"When my father learned I had become a Christian, he beat me, kicked me out on the streets, and told me never to return." Abebe's voice held a trace of old sadness.

"How old were you?" I frowned. I'd never get used to hearing such stories about children anywhere. Though my family had not been super religious or wealthy, we'd always had God and enough to eat. I could not imagine my dad being so upset with me that he'd kick me out on the street. And there was no circumstance I could imagine where I would do that to any of my children.

"I was a teenager. Maybe fourteen? I spent many years surviving, if you can call it that, on the streets. Sometimes, I dressed up and disguised myself as an older man, hoping no one would harass or beat me because old men are respected and left alone. Often, all I had to eat was a few packs of sugar I could find at one of the restaurants."

"That's a hard life." I learned that words often seemed lacking when talking to people in Ethiopia. A lot of what I said seemed inadequate for the situations we encountered.

"It was." He nodded, not seeming to mind my questions or lack of profound thoughts. "Life was tough. I barely survived."

"How did you end up here? Working with the orphans?" It was a hard jump to imagine. The more I knew about Abebe, the more he impressed me.

"The hardships I experienced while living on the streets motivated me to pursue an education. I ended up working many years for the government as a Hydrogeologist." He didn't brag, but I knew from others that he was incredibly successful. He'd recently quit his job when the mission organization Ben served asked him to be the director of the orphanages and adoption ministry.

"God called me to serve the country's orphans, widows, and poor," he said humbly, leaving out all the rest as if titles and recognition meant nothing compared to being of service in some way to the people. His love for the widows and orphans and his strong, radiant faith shone brightly. Even shy Aliyah smiled around him, tucking her tiny hand into his trustingly. She was the only little girl in the orphanage. Timid and unsure about us Westerners, she kept her distance.

"She is five but small for her age," Abebe said when I asked about her. "Truly a sweet little soul."

She watched us from afar, and occasionally, when I caught her eye, she'd smile shyly.

"Aliyah and her grandma have a special bond, together at different ends of life," Abebe told me.

Of all the widows I met, Aliyah's grandma stood out. She was warm, loving, and funny. Though well over eighty years old when I met her, she had a strength of spirit forged by a long life of extreme hardship and loss that made her appreciate every day.

When the time came to say goodbye, a quiet certainty settled over me—I would never see them again. I lingered, unwilling to leave, a knot tightening in my chest. Parting felt like losing something I couldn't name. As we climbed into the van, the weight in my heart grew heavier with each step, pulling me down as the distance between us stretched into something final.

Everyone gathered around. Children and widows sang and waved as we left the compound, and more than one person in our little group cried. My heart flooded with conflicting emotions, and my mind whirled with unorganized thoughts, trying to process everything I'd seen and experienced.

The beauty of Ethiopia stunned me as much as the loss and sadness. My insides twisted as I listened to the happy songs the kids sang when we pulled away. I smiled back into smiling faces but wondered what good my visit would do. Will it serve a lasting purpose beyond my fond memories? *What will become of Joshua, Aliyah, and the other children?*

The drive back to the hotel blurred, but the ache of leaving stayed sharp, echoing long after we'd gone. As I pondered, heart heavy, we drove along bumpy roads back into the city where comfortable Western things waited to bring me back to my everyday life. I asked Abebe if Joshua and Aliyah had families waiting to adopt them.

"No," he said, shaking his head sadly. "I wish it were otherwise, but older children have few options. No one will take them. Aliyah can stay until her grandmother passes on, then..." Abebe trailed off as if not wishing to illuminate the options remaining for the young girl after that.

It's the same in America; older children struggle to find anyone to love or care for them who is willing to commit to forever. People want babies, I learned when we adopted older children.

I couldn't stop thinking about Joshua and Aliyah and the terrible things that might happen to them. *Why did God lead me to them if not to help?*

Chapter Three

Surrendered to the Depths

Over the next few days, our group visited several widow and orphan homes. The stories were the same everywhere we went—destitute older women and young children with no one to care for them. Without the widows' and orphans' homes, they would be left on the streets to beg. The homes were lifeboats in a sea of desperation and hopelessness.

Exhausted physically from the lack of sleep and jet lag and emotionally from the overwhelming scenes of despair, the sad and heartbreaking stories soon overwhelmed me. Every child in the orphanages we visited experienced profound loss—loss of family, loss of food, loss of hope. Americans, even our poorest, have so much by comparison.

I struggled to understand the imbalance between my world of abundance and wealth and this one of such hopelessness and misery. *Why does God watch it all and do nothing?*

I prayed for Him to show me the way forward in His wisdom. To teach me through those I met and those who walked with me on this journey to help the orphans of Ethiopia.

Though the good the mission was doing was clear, it was hard to see the problem through American eyes and not also see that the mission's efforts were not enough. Far too many children suffered here. Way more than I'd been prepared for in far more dire circumstances. Surely, someone could find a solution to help more than a precious few of the people served by the mission.

Why don't more people help? Doesn't anybody care? Don't they see the suffering children filling up the streets? My heart became overwhelmed with questions I had no answers for. Feeling defeated and beaten, I slept fitfully on my final night in Addis Ababa.

***

We visited one last orphanage, bringing bags of clothes and other donations from the U.S., playing with the children, and holding tiny babies starved for affection and attention.

I showed a group of excited children pictures of animals in a book, sitting with them in a circle on the cool ceramic tiled floor. Later, I watched a man holding a small child in his arms, with two other children clinging to his legs, talk somberly to the home's director.

Fukado was his name, Abebe told me. "He lost his wife to HIV and tuberculosis. Both are still frequent killers in underdeveloped countries like Ethiopia. Fukado is a hod carrier," he explained, "He brings mud to bricklayers. It's a very menial day-labor job and certainly not enough income to feed himself and three children. Despite Fukado's best efforts, he can no longer care for and provide for his children without his wife's added income. The children have not eaten in three days, and this is not the first time."

The man's story sent sadness stabbing through me like a spear. Even when I was starting out, fresh out of high school and in the Army, I'd never gone hungry. Not feeding my children for days was unimaginable.

"When one parent dies in an extremely low-income family like this one, it is catastrophic. The family disintegrates within days. Children become orphaned without help. Jobs are not easy to come by and pay little," Abebe said. "There is literally no help for him anywhere. He has come to the orphanage because it's his last hope. He knows his children won't make it if he doesn't do something."

"Desperate and hopeless parents drown in poverty. They know they won't make it but don't want their children to drown with them. The orphanage is a lifeboat that can take their children to a safe harbor, albeit possibly in some foreign land away from them forever. They see this as a far better and only option for their survival. Without help or resources, they can do only one thing—decide, grounded in the sacrificial love of a desperate father or mother who will do the unthinkable to save their children—to give them up," Abonesh told us. "We help as many as we can but must turn many away."

My heart hurt for this man I did not know and others like him. He hugged his little ones for the last time, not knowing what would happen to them when he walked away and left them with strangers.

He'll never see them again.

I watched the scene unfold in shock.

The nannies embraced the little ones who cried out for their daddy long after he was no longer in sight.

"What will happen to them now?" I asked as soft-spoken ladies led the children away.

"The orphanage will care for them, hoping that a family from the U.S. or Europe will adopt them," Abebe explained.

These children were orphans due to circumstances beyond anyone's control. I couldn't comprehend the lack of any other solution for the father, unable to put myself in Fukado's shoes. There were so many layers between me and the place he'd found himself in that I could not imagine it. My heart, too, would not hold the thought of leaving any of my children behind for too long. The pain of even the thought was too much. My eyes filled with tears.

"This can't be happening." I shook my head as if confused that my money, desire to help, and optimism couldn't somehow change things. I had never faced such problems before. Many before me had come and failed to find a solution, but still, I felt I must try.

"Many children in impoverished countries end up in orphanages because their parents simply can't feed them. They have nothing. Nothing," Ben said. I heard the emotion in his voice and knew he struggled with the same emotions I did. The same feelings of hopelessness and sadness.

"Some people must sell their children to others who then take them to foreign countries to work as slave laborers in factories or in the sex trade. At least here, these kids have a chance," Abebe said. "At least here, there is hope for some."

"There is so much I didn't know," I said, my voice softer as I faced things I didn't want to learn. The idea that many of the orphans I'd met had at least one parent who had to do the unthinkable, just like Fukado, and leave them to the fates unsettled me in a way I still have a tough time thinking about. The idea that these people once lived in thriving towns and made a fair wage, living full, happy lives before tragedy struck, was hard to grasp, considering the conditions everywhere we went. Such poverty and extreme need were impossible to grasp even when looking right at it.

I constantly thought about my six kids back home. What if something forced me to abandon them? Did Fukado love his children any less than I love mine? Did he love them more? Would I do the unthinkable for my children's survival in his shoes? No matter how hard I tried, I could never imagine being in the same position. Not with the options I would have between family and friends, programs and charities, and the church and county. Imagining every lifeline I took for granted gone overwhelmed me. I wanted to talk to Fukado to find a way to fix things, but he was long gone. I would never see him or his children again.

Crushed, but before I could think much more about how I felt, Abonesh invited us to join the home director when she sat with two older boys.

"These boys have been at the orphanage for a long time," she explained. "They will soon age out."

That didn't sound good.

She spoke with the boys in Amharic, Ethiopia's common language, with the help of an interpreter.

I had to wait for interpretation, but I could tell that whatever she said was good news, and I was relieved. The boys smiled from ear to ear, and one burst into tears.

Abonesh said, "A family from the United States is adopting them."

The director shared details about the family, showed them a picture book the family made for the boys, and gave them gifts of new clothes and many other American items like cookies and backpacks, puzzles, and comic books. Finally, they received beautiful blankets in the Ethiopian colors of red, yellow, and green from the mission, which Abebe wrapped around them.

"These blankets are embroidered with scripture. 'For I know the plans I have for you, declares the Lord, plans for welfare and not for evil, to give you a future and a hope,'" Abebe said, wiping away tears that flowed freely.

"Local women make them with donated supplies, earning enough to keep their children from places like this," the director said. "Even still, they gift them to the children here to pay forward what they received."

"Just by selling blankets, these women make enough to feed their kids?" I felt the spark of an idea.

"And send them to school in shoes. It's very different here. Extraordinarily little is needed to make money enough to care for a family," the director said.

The boys seemed overwhelmed and extremely happy, crying and hugging one another and us for a long time.

Most of us cried, too. We'd seen so much sadness and loss. But here was joy and hope. In this place of contrast, things changed quickly, from no hope to a future.

These memories lingered with me—the remarkable children, the plight of the widows, and the remarkable souls I encountered changed me forever, but as the van rumbled toward the airport, the heaviness in my heart remained. I stared out the window, watching the exotic landscape blur past.

How could I go home to my comfortable life as if this place didn't exist?

Joshua and Aliyah's smiles haunted me.

Experiencing such suffering, up close and personal, has messed me up. *But what about the children? What of them?*

The ache of leaving the orphans behind stirred something deeper, something I hadn't allowed myself to think about in a long time—the quiet, unresolved longing, hope, and heartbreak that marked years of trying unsuccessfully to have children and build a family with Chris. I thought I'd buried it. But now, the memories surfaced, tugging me back to the start. Before Africa. Before any of this.

Chapter Four

God Asks for an Answer

I sat behind Crystal, a stunningly beautiful girl who would later become my wife, in 11th-grade math class. Tall and slender, her hazel eyes held depth and wisdom beyond her years. Her warm smile could brighten the dreariest of days.

From our first conversation, I sensed a profound shift in me—a stirring of my heart that transcended mere infatuation. It was as if God orchestrated our meeting, igniting a spark that grew into our enduring love.

We married the year after we graduated high school.

Life seemed simple, although I now see, with a clarity I didn't have as a younger man, that our lives were often complicated as we tried to figure out how to be adults.

We thought we'd have a few kids, maybe two or three like everybody else, but after our first daughter Brittany was born soon into our marriage that didn't happen. This went on for about ten years. It seemed like everyone could get pregnant, but not us.

Chris prayed, "God. Either fulfill this desire to have more children or take it away from me. This is too painful to bear."

I wasn't as patient with God or the process and doctors, poking and prodding. One day, driving somewhere by myself, angry and sad after another failed infertility procedure, I yelled at God for not answering our prayers when it seemed like everyone around me had no trouble building a family. "Why God? Why are you not answering our prayers? I don't understand! It's not too big for you to give us more children. Why does it seem like you let everyone else get pregnant easily enough? Do you not care? Lord, if I could ask for one thing in life, it would be to have more children. That's all I am asking. Is that too hard for you?"

I struggled to understand why God didn't answer our prayers, and I tried to find excuses for Him. Maybe God was delaying, preparing us for something, knowing better than we did what was coming. Or perhaps the point was to learn patience or trust. I gave up trying to figure it out since there seemed to be no clear answer.

Since then, I've learned that God usually answers prayers, though seldom how we expect or even ask for. This was no exception; God prepared us for far more than we ever dreamed or bargained for. After almost twelve years of knocking on a closed door, Chris suggested we knock on a different door, hitting me with it as soon as I came home from work one afternoon. "Why don't we look into adoption?"

I hadn't thought about it a lot before, though I was open to the idea. My dad was adopted, but we didn't talk about that when I was growing up. Chris's grandmother raised her after she lost both her parents as a child. Though she rarely spoke about her experiences, they'd turned her into a loving caregiver devoted to her family and friends.

"Why do you think we should consider adoption now, honey?" I asked.

"I've thought about it off and on," she said, "but I wanted to make sure that, in my heart, adoption was not plan B. I wanted peace, knowing that adoption is God's plan A for us." Her beautiful hazel eyes shimmered with emotion.

They say God opens a window when he closes a door. Was this the window? Were we to look out and see His different plans to enlarge our family? I was excited to explore the possibility. Chris set out to find out what she could about the entire process while I happily tagged along, with no idea where the adoption journey would take us.

For the first time in a long time, we stopped praying for things to be different. We went along with whatever God had in store, learning that you invest your whole heart and lots of time, questions, paperwork, and prayers in the adoption process. After a whirlwind experience, many heart-wrenching months later, we were blessed with the adoption of a beautiful baby boy. We named him Matthew, which means God's gift. The depth of our love for him and our bond was beyond words. He brought so much joy into our lives from the moment he arrived.

The next few years passed quickly. We learned more about the adoption process, a blessed but challenging road, attending seminars and conferences to learn and better equip ourselves in this new world. We participated in a conference where families had children from every country and race with special needs. The diversity, love, and bonds these families created through adoption inspired me.

In the car after the conference, I asked Chris, "Do you think we could adopt a child of color?" I asked, knowing how hard it was for agencies to find families for these children.

"Of course, we could!" she said, like she was insulted I'd implied she might say no.

Thirty days after that brief conversation, a birth mother chose us to adopt her newborn, a beautiful African American baby boy. Chris and I couldn't have been happier. We named him Andrew and loved him instantly.

Sometimes, I think that what happened next was God showing off, just throwing in something extra special to make me sit up and take notice of His goodness and power.

We went to court and finalized Andrew's adoption when he was five months old. Later that day, I was in my home office when Chris came in. She rarely bothered me when I was working; when she did, it was something worth interrupting me about. This time was no exception.

The odd look on her face alarmed me instantly. "What's wrong?"

"Do you have any pregnancy tests?" she asked softly.

"Pregnancy tests?" I'd transitioned into a career in medical sales, so the question wasn't that odd, and I did have such samples available. "Why?"

"It sounds crazy, but I think I might be pregnant." Her eyes were round with wonder.

"That's crazy." I rummaged through my samples and gave Chris a pregnancy test, anxiously waiting while she went into the bathroom.

"What does the test show?" I asked, pacing.

"Give me a minute!" she yelled through the door.

There's no way she's pregnant, I thought.

"It's positive," she said, emerging white-faced from the bathroom several minutes later. She showed me the pink line on the stick that clearly said positive.

"No way. It's wrong, right?" It's not that I didn't want it to be true; I didn't believe it was possible.

"Give me another one." She held out her hand.

I gave her a different brand. "Try this kind. The other one must be defective."

It took a while, but she returned, and this time, we waited together until the test showed another positive.

Whispering like she didn't want to jinx it, Chris said, "We're having a baby."

I didn't know what to think, though joy spread as I accepted that the impossible had happened. "How? It's been seventeen years since Brittany was born. We haven't used birth control all this time, and nothing. All the infertility procedures we tried. Why now?"

"And on the day we finalized Andrew's adoption!" Chris grinned. "Seems like a miracle to me."

We hugged one another closely. "The very same day," I said incredulously. "Wild!"

"Crazy!" Chris grinned, glowing with happiness and wonder.

We talked about how we'd tell our friends and family. "They'll be so surprised!" Chris said.

"Not as much as us." I thought of my prayers so long ago and how I'd begged God for a son, only to be reminded that things like timing and plans are better left to Him, who knows best. What would happen would happen, and not according to my will.

Soon, our new baby girl arrived. We named her KayliAnna.

Chris and I remained shocked that we'd had another baby. Everyone else was too. People often joked, "I guess Chris was finally able to relax after adopting, and that's why she became pregnant."

Chris would roll her eyes and reply, "Do you really think I couldn't relax at any point over the last seventeen years?"

We knew God's plan for our family included having children by both adoption and by birth. But after four children—two boys and two girls—I thought we were done having kids. Four seemed like a good, even number.

I was wrong again.

Although she was over the moon about having another baby, Chris still had a huge heart for adoption, so giving birth didn't mean we were done adopting. Three years after KayliAnna was born, we adopted another beautiful baby girl and named her Jayna. We couldn't have been more thrilled and amazed that a beautiful African American birthmother entrusted her precious baby to us to raise, love, and care for. Despite her difficulties and challenges, she saw beyond the cultural and racial differences and chose us to adopt her child.

Through each adoption journey, we have been humbled and blessed by the sacrificial love it takes to place a child for adoption.

Another year quickly passed. As we caught our breath with our little brood of five kids, we received a call from the adoption agency again. When Jayna was sixteen months old, we welcomed little Adalyn into our family.

Suddenly, never having imagined our lives would look like this, we were a family of six kids.

People asked us about the challenges of raising so many children. They said things like, "Are you done now?" and "You sure have your hands full."

We became used to the shocked, bewildered, and amazed reactions when people first met us. Apparently, one kid was normal, but six was nuts!

By the time Adalyn joined our family, we'd been married twenty-three years. Our lives were full with six kids—a nice, even number once again.

We loved our chaotic, full life and our unique, diverse family and had our hands full for the next several years. So, this time, I thought our new additions would be the last.

Of course, I had no idea what life had for us next. God was just warming up.

"Did you ever picture our lives like this when we met in high school?" Chris asked one night as we drifted off to sleep.

"Not even close." I laughed, turning toward her.

She nodded into my chest as if she knew exactly what I meant. "Life's a lot different from when we started, that's for sure."

Before drifting off to sleep, I reflected on my childhood and adulthood. *How did I survive and become who I am now?* I went down memory lane—so many rough patches and wrong roads full of pain, fear, and regret—and I felt immense sorrow as I reflected on my younger self. I'd been so lost, so hurt, afraid, and hiding, unable to deal with my feelings. All the destructive behaviors only sparked more anxiety and confusion. But so much had changed in my life since those troubling teenage years. *Where would my life be now without His intervention?* I shuddered to think what it would look like. Chris and I often said we wouldn't still be married if it wasn't for God. We didn't say that lightly because we knew the truth of it all too well.

That night, my last thought before I drifted off to sleep, holding my sleeping wife tight, was how incredibly thankful I was for God's deliverance. My life was amazing and complete, though often overwhelming. At that moment, everything felt right—like the pieces had finally fallen into place. But life has a way of shifting when you least expect it, testing the foundations you thought were solid. As it turned out, the next chapter was nothing like I'd imagined.

***

My experiences and encounters in Ethiopia left an indelible mark on my soul, altering my perspective and understanding of the world when I returned home. I viewed life through a new lens, with a heightened awareness and a deeper appreciation for the diversity of human experiences, though my thoughts were unsettled and my heart weary.

It hit me hardest when I walked back into our new, custom-built home nestled into five lovely, tree-filled acres. This was our dream home, with a sports court, lots of property for the kids to run and play, and enough room for everyone. We'd spent the last year building it for my growing family of six, but as I put down my bags, all I could see were the contrasts I'd witnessed in Africa. The house seemed excessive, larger than the biggest orphanage I'd visited, and furnished with all the modern conveniences, beautiful custom trim, and décor. The knickknacks seemed too many, and the furniture too ornate. Even the chandelier in the dining room that had seemed perfect before I'd left seemed too big and flashy now. I wondered what a difference any of these things would make in the lives of the people I met in Ethiopia.

My heart warmed quickly, being with Chris and the children again. It seemed like I'd been gone for years and that my journey had taken me far away in miles, heart, and soul.

I settled back in the way one always does after a vacation, no matter how epic, enjoying every minute of my homecoming. I tried to stay in the moment and not think about work and obligations. Still, my mind had already turned from the horrors I'd witnessed, the problem too great, and my usual responsibilities too many.

The kids eagerly crowded around when I opened my suitcases to reveal gifts I'd picked especially for them. Exotic little wood carvings of giraffes and elephants, animals I hadn't seen in Ethiopia but unique and delightful to my wildlife-loving kids, were a hit. I brought beautifully colored dresses and blankets for Chris and the girls.

After a catch-up dinner, during which the kids and Chris told me everything I missed while I was away, and I spoke only of the fantastic people and country I'd seen and of my travels, the kids went to bed and to study.

I finally sat and relaxed alone with Chris in front of a fire in our cheery, oversized hearth.

"You must be exhausted," Chris said, rubbing my shoulders.

"I'm tired," I admitted, closing my eyes. "The flight home seemed endless, but there's so much I want to share with you."

Back then, it wasn't easy to make calls back home. Smartphones and WIFI had not been invented yet, so I couldn't update her during the trip. I was dying to unpack everything but didn't know where to begin. It seemed too much to unload onto another person, even one who loved me as much as Chris. My trip was horrible and unthinkable. Hopeless and sad. Not at all the trip we'd talked about before I left, though surely Chris had to know I would see poverty and sad conditions.

"I'm listening," she said.

Though I wasn't usually one to talk about my feelings a lot, that was all it took for me to start, right from the first horror—the barefoot beggar woman on the corner who'd grabbed my arm. I didn't get far before I broke down emotionally, trying to find words to tell her about the children in the orphanages and on the streets. I tried to hold back nothing, but I could only cry and speak in bursts of the horrors I'd witnessed and the hopelessness of it all.

When I stopped, Chris hugged me. "You haven't had time to absorb the trip fully. It's okay. Things will be clearer in the morning."

"They already are." I squeezed her hand, calmer and more centered after talking with her. She was right. It would take time to sort through my emotions and thoughts about my African experiences.

I told her about Joshua and Aliyah, smiling the whole time. My heart was warm with the memories of the first time Aliyah shyly smiled at me, letting me read her a book about colorful bears who wished they were brown. "You would not believe the smiles on these two kids! Their whole faces open up and beam happiness. Joshua takes such pride in helping the widows do daily things. And even though Aliyah is quiet and shy, she is so sweet once you get to know her. Those two really stole my heart."

As I remembered the children playing, their laughter rising like a song on the breeze, a bittersweet joy tugged at me. Something in their freedom unsettled me, reflecting what I had spent years trying to control—life unfolding on its own terms. I smiled at the thought, but beneath it, an old tension stirred, a memory of when I stood before God, demanding that He fit my plans and bend to my timing. I had pushed so hard to shape my life, blind to the truth that I was running from my fears, terrified of surrendering to what I couldn't control.

Shortly after we adopted Adalyn, I went out for my usual run, earphones in, music blaring, my legs moving effortlessly beneath me. The rhythm felt good, steady. I was in my zone. Then, without warning, something happened that I've only experienced a few times. I heard the voice of God—not audibly, but unmistakably, deep in my heart. It cut through the music, and I couldn't understand why He would choose that moment to speak to me. I had already spent time in prayer that morning. As far as I was concerned, we were good for the day.

"Do you want me to bless your life?" God asked.

The question pierced my heart. I didn't waste time wondering whether this was God's voice—I knew it was. But, after blessing my life so much up to this point, why would He ask me such an easy question?

Before I could answer, God spoke again, hitting me with the truth that rocked me to my core. "I wish you would stop telling Me how to bless your life and be open to what I have for you," He said.

I was stunned to realize I hadn't been open to what God had for me, what He wanted to give me, or how He wanted to bless me. I had tried to influence God, put Him in my little box of blessings, and control Him like a genie in a bottle. He was right. I hadn't opened myself to what He had for me and my future.

God's words penetrated my soul. Breathing deeply on the side of the road, I rested my hands on my knees and pondered His truth bomb. Then, I turned around and ran home, my mind spinning.

Sitting with Chris in the kitchen, where we always seem to end up when we have something serious to discuss, I told her what God said. "I believe I heard the truth about my life and wanting to control God. From now on, I want to be open to what God wants for me and our family."

I vowed never again to tell God how He should bless me. That day marked a turning point—a quiet but seismic shift in how I approached my faith. I no longer cling to the illusion of control, trying to shape divine will into my desires. Instead, I opened my hands and heart to receive whatever He had in store, trusting the path would be far more intricate and beautiful than anything I could envision.

Chris's smile was soft but knowing, her eyes shimmering with a depth that said everything we never needed to put into words. She understood. We were bound together by love and the quiet strength of surrender. Whatever storms lay ahead, we would face them together.

***

The reality of my promise settled in ways neither of us could have predicted. There would be life-changing, soul-stretching decisions that would redefine everything we thought we wanted. Conversations we hadn't yet had about family and purpose would soon unfold. And the thought that kept resurfacing—about children, about giving our love and our lives to those who needed it most—began to grow louder.

I hadn't planned on it, but somehow, I knew. My heart was drawn beyond myself to a new kind of love. And it was already shaping our future, even as I unknowingly prepared for what was to come.

I hadn't gone to Africa planning to adopt, but something stirred in me there, something profound and inevitable. Within days of my homecoming, Chris and I considered what it would take to adopt Joshua and Aliyah. But first, we discussed the possibility of adopting children from Ethiopia with our children.

"We have more than enough room in our home and hearts for more children to become part of our family," Chris said, sharing how I'd met the kids we hoped would soon become their brothers and sisters.

The kids were thrilled, and we began the adoption process a few days later.

Though happy about this, I still struggled to process and make sense of all I had seen in Ethiopia.

"I just can't reconcile my comfortable, successful life with the poverty and brokenness in Africa," I said to Chris one night after the kids went to bed.

"Keep praying on it and trust that God will make it clear exactly what He wants you and us to do. We know He is leading us to adopt Aliyah and Joshua. Let's take one step at a time and trust Him for the future."

I knew there was more to it than that, but I figured she was probably right, so I settled in and focused on the process of adopting the two kids, keeping my worries to myself, and trying to plan for all the changes about to come for our new family of eight kids.

***

Months later, on the plane to Africa, on our trip to bring home Joshua and Aliyah, I pondered the changes we were about to experience. Everything in my life was expanding again, along with my family and desire to do more to help those in need.

"People think we're crazy," I told Chris, who sat in the aisle seat next to a blessedly empty middle seat between us.

"Maybe we are." She laughed.

"Life is good. Crazy or not," I said. Though raising such a large family often presented challenges, I'd learned to balance my responsibilities as a father with work and my desire to help those in need. I felt much better than I had when this journey began. "I'm so excited to head back to Ethiopia with you." I tried to focus on the good while preparing her for the bad.

Chris's tear-filled eyes said everything as she saw many of the same sad sights I did a year earlier. I could see her heart spilling over with love and compassion for the broken people everywhere. Because of the loss of her parents as a young girl, she understood the pain when children lost their parents in a way I never could.

Still, despite the sadness, our trip was filled with many good moments, and I loved experiencing the people's beauty and culture through Chris's eyes.

We traveled to the orphanage to pick up Aliyah and Joshua the day after we arrived. The memory of our first talk about adopting them felt distant yet curiously prophetic as we stood on foreign soil together. Surrounded by faces that carried the weight of loss and resilience, I realized that our lives had taken a turn neither of us could have imagined. Among the children, wide-eyed and hopeful despite their circumstances, was a future we hadn't planned for but could no longer deny.

"There are so many children, and always more arriving. Like most orphanages in Ethiopia, ours is full of children hoping to be adopted or in the process of being adopted," the orphanage director told us.

"It's heartbreaking to see so many children in need of families, to know many have been here for so many years." Chris's expressive eyes worried that no one would ever come for these other children, that they would never become part of a new family.

"Today is the day we've prayed about for over a year," I reminded her, taking her hand. "The day we take our two kids from here and return home."

One of the widows brought Joshua and Aliyah out to us. Chris approached them slowly, then crouched down with outstretched arms.

Joshua and Aliyah hesitated, their eyes meeting mine momentarily, before looking back to this woman they had only seen in a picture and going to her shyly.

We could not fully prepare them for what would happen. Their world would change forever from this day forward. Still, we tried staying in a modest guesthouse with Aliyah and Joshua. At the same time, we waited for the final paperwork to be processed, the last official step before we could bring them home. Those days, though brief, gave us time to bond, a quiet interlude in the whirlwind of change.

Once we were back home, with our lives finally settling into a new rhythm, I reflected on how much my heart had transformed over the past year. A calm sense of certainty replaced the restlessness I hadn't even realized existed. My first trip to Ethiopia opened my eyes to the beauty of the country and the deep love I felt for these two children the moment I met them. Over time, it became clear that God was calling me in a new direction.

For years, I had served in church leadership, eventually stepping into the role of pastor—a calling I had cherished deeply. But those trips to Ethiopia broadened my perspective. I began to see the world beyond the walls of our church, and with that expanded vision came a growing sense that my role was shifting. I couldn't shake the feeling that God had something else in store for me, and slowly, I started to think about stepping down as pastor. I prayed for guidance, trusting God would reveal His plan in time.

Our days were filled with joy and challenges as we adjusted to life with Aliyah and Joshua. Neither of them spoke a word of English, and we didn't know Amharic. Yet, somehow, we communicated, piecing together a new language as a family. Thankfully, they both quickly adapted to American food—Aliyah, especially, developed an unexpected love for pizza.

As I watched our family grow close, my heart swelled with gratitude. These children were now a part of us, forever. Yet even amid this joy, there was a quiet tug at my spirit, a sense that my work wasn't finished.

They say that when the time is right, opportunities present themselves. And so it was. One day, the mission organization that had taken me to Ethiopia on that first life-altering trip reached out. They asked me to join their leadership team, to travel and speak on behalf of the widows and orphans, sharing their stories at churches and conferences. The invitation felt like the answer to a question I hadn't fully formed yet. I accepted without hesitation, knowing this was God's new direction for me. I would be a voice for the voiceless.

Life took on a new rhythm—one filled with the noise and energy of eight children and a renewed focus on raising awareness for those experiencing poverty, for the widows and orphans whose voices were so often unheard. My days were busy, but they were rich with purpose.

Raising eight children, stepping into this new role, and carrying the expectations of those around me were more than I had prepared for. And then there were the fears, creeping in quietly during the stillness of the night. I kept moving forward, but deep inside, I wondered if I was walking toward a future I wasn't equipped to handle.

Chapter Five

Searching for a Bridge

I buried the anxiety under layers of busyness, throwing myself into work, the adoption, the ministry, and the endless responsibilities of family life, anything to keep from facing what was gnawing at me. I had always believed I could push through, that faith and determination would be enough. But now, with so many people relying on me and my mind fraying at the edges, I realized I was on the brink of something I couldn't ignore, a breakdown that had been building, hidden beneath my refusal to ask for help.

Maybe it wasn't the first time I'd avoided reaching out. I hadn't asked for advice when I joined the Army straight out of high school either, driven more by a restless urgency than any real plan. Back then, the weight of being a newly married man made the future uncertain, and the Army seemed like a way to carve out a path forward.

My first assignment took me to Fort Bliss, Texas, where Chris and I were suddenly far from anything familiar. We had no friends, no family nearby, just each other and the walls of our tiny studio apartment. Our world was small then, as small as the space we called home, but we didn't mind. We were young and in love, and the unknown felt like an adventure we were ready to take on together. I thought I could handle anything life threw at me, that if I just kept moving forward, it would all work out. I didn't realize, even then, how easily I could confuse action with progress, how I was already starting to bury the deeper anxieties that would follow me into the years ahead.

Starting a marriage with the pressures of the Army was hard. My technical school training lasted an entire year (so much for not wanting to do more school after high school). Chris and I were just two kids deeply in love but mostly clueless about living as newlyweds in a new place, figuring everything out ourselves.

Tech school was fast-paced and demanding, and I sometimes struggled to keep up. The pressure to perform weighed heavily, and I didn't always manage it gracefully. The stress seeped into my young marriage, straining what was already fragile. I often wanted to escape, go out drinking with the guys, and leave Chris alone in our tiny apartment. Naturally, this didn't sit well with her, and our first year was marked by arguments caused mainly by my immaturity and selfishness.

I knew something was missing in those moments, but I couldn't figure out what it was. I wasn't thriving, and deep down, I knew I was failing—not just at school but at life in general. It left me unsettled, like I was drifting without a clear direction. There was a sense of hope when I finished tech school and received orders for Fort Lewis, Washington. Neither of us had ever been to the Pacific Northwest. Starting fresh in a new place felt like the reset we desperately needed.

As we made our way up the Pacific Coast, we stopped to stay with Chris's sister and her family for a few days. During that brief visit, amidst the ordinary chaos of family life, we received the news that would change everything: we were having a baby. The weight of it hit us in waves—barely adults ourselves, and now, we were about to step into the daunting role of parenthood. We couldn't have been more thrilled or terrified.

After arriving in Washington, we searched for a home near Fort Lewis. Still struggling financially on Army pay, we had limited options but found a one-bedroom cracker box of a house about the size of our studio apartment in El Paso. We were excited about our new place but still trying to figure out how to be adults and what married life was all about.

Though life was moving forward on the surface, inside, I was still unraveling—filled with a relentless mix of anxiety, anger, and a deep, aching emptiness. Something was wrong, but I couldn't put a name to it. It felt as though I was slowly drowning, even as everything around me suggested I should be thriving. Things were going well, and life was good. Chris and I had everything we needed. The future should have looked bright, young, in love, and enjoying our new baby girl, but a sense of unease followed me.

I've learned you can't hide from the lessons God wants you to learn, and the feelings I suppressed for years eventually caught up with me.

***

At an annual national sales meeting months after adopting Joshua and Aliyah, I sat at a lavish banquet table, celebrating alongside my colleagues. I had just been awarded the highest sales honor of the year. On the outside, everything seemed perfect—smiles, handshakes, champagne. But inside, the weight of everything I had tried to ignore was finally bearing down, threatening to crush me.

Sitting in that grand ballroom, surrounded by the finest food and the best-dressed people, I couldn't stop thinking about Ethiopia. The images of overwhelming poverty, children with hollow eyes, and the raw desperation I had seen on my trips haunted me. It was impossible to reconcile these two worlds—the abundance of my American life and the despair I had witnessed overseas. Here I was, celebrating in a room draped in opulence while so many around the world fought for mere survival. Why was I sitting here, surrounded by luxury, when they had nothing? Why was I so blessed when others were trapped in unimaginable suffering?

I excused myself from the table, slipping away from the celebration and into a darkened meeting room down a long hall. I needed to be alone, away from the noise, to think. I felt like a man out of place, caught between two worlds, neither of which felt like home. I had been so determined to succeed, to prove myself, but now, in the quiet of that room, I wondered what any of it was worth.

I sat in the darkness, the glow from the ballroom still faintly visible through the crack in the door and thought about the orphans I'd met in Ethiopia. I had wanted to feel like I was making a difference—not just for Joshua and Aliyah, but for all the children like them. But that night, the truth hit me: I had been fooling myself, thinking I could somehow mend the world's brokenness by bringing two children into my home. That wasn't how it worked.

How could I help the orphans, the widows, and those trapped in poverty when I couldn't even help myself?

The success I had chased for so long suddenly felt hollow.

I wasn't just overwhelmed by the world's brokenness but by my own shallowness.

I could no longer turn away from the cries of the poor and the orphans I had witnessed. The images of poverty and brokenness were now a part of me, shaping how I saw the world. My time in that other reality had changed me irrevocably—I knew I could never feel truly at home in the comfort and prosperity I once took for granted.

"Help me understand, God. How can these two worlds fit together? I cannot reconcile the contrasts. I don't understand why all this goodness is happening to me. What am I to do with all this success or these feelings that won't go away no matter what I do? Please show me the way. There must be a greater reason for the blessings you have showered on my life than just for myself and my family. Please show me what to do. I'm open to what you have for me," I prayed, returning to my waiting friends, leaving the problem to God again.

***

Surrounded by the comforts of American life, memories of Ethiopia continued to linger in my unsettled mind. They made the contrast between my privileged existence and the harsh realities of life for the people I met in Africa disturbing, causing me to question even more the depth of my values, priorities, and faith. The familiar comforts of home seemed hollow and superficial, everything abundant or joyful overshadowed by my soul-stirring encounters in Ethiopia. Grappling with unsettling thoughts that challenged my deepest held beliefs, I couldn't get the crying young mother's face out of my mind. "What are you going to do?" she asked me every day.

I couldn't forget her. The young mother's eyes followed me for months after I left Korah. I saw her face in my dreams—her silent cry for help echoing in the quiet moments when I thought I could push it all away. What haunted me most wasn't just her poverty or the hunger in her child's eyes. It was the knowledge that I had nothing to give her. The realization that I, who had so much, had walked away from someone with nothing.

And in my darkest moments, when the doubts crept in, her face reminded me: I couldn't fix the world, but there had to be a way to help people before things reached this point.

That silent plea and desperate look became the seed for something bigger. As her image haunted me, the idea grew. If we could find ways to reach people before they fell into such despair, families were torn apart, and children became orphans, we could make a difference.

The question wasn't how to help her at that moment. It was how to prevent that moment from happening in the first place.

I didn't understand the problems enough to think of a single workable solution to solve poverty like I'd seen. Troubled and overwhelmed by the magnitude of the situation, I prayed. "God help me understand. I don't know what to do. Show me the way forward."

"I can't reconcile what I saw, Ben," I told my friend, knowing he'd understand, over lunch at work one day. I'd just closed a big deal with a long-term client and was grappling again with that feeling of unfairness I seemed to carry daily. "The disparity of everything, I mean. We have so much. Simple things like running water. Drawers full of silverware. Toilets. A fridge that always has food in it. Coffee filters. Stupid things like straws and plastic bags and air fresheners." Everything I had piled up in my mind, overflowing. "I don't know what to do."

"Don't be so hard on yourself. It's hard to imagine what it's like before you go and it takes time when you get back," Ben said. "You do what you can. That's all any of us can do."

Chris told me much the same thing. Time heals all wounds. But for weeks, I had nightmares and intrusive, near-constant thoughts of the people I'd left to suffer, like a form of PTSD that was always with me, triggering my own long-held anxieties.

Chris's words were meant to comfort me, but I couldn't quiet the storm inside me. I knew she meant well, but no amount of logic or reassurance could make sense of the disparity I carried with me every day. It wasn't just about running water, silverware, or air fresheners. It was the weight of knowing that while I lived in abundance, so many lived in suffering. I tried to move forward and told myself that time would help, as Chris kept reminding me, but the truth was, it wasn't getting better. The nightmares still came—images of faces I couldn't forget, voices I couldn't silence. Haunted by everything I left undone. The intrusive thoughts and endless anxiety followed me everywhere, a constant reminder of how far I was from making any real difference. And so, in the darkest moments, I wondered if there was any way out of my helplessness. But then, one night, when the weight of it all seemed too much to bear, I had a dream. It was unlike anything before—a spark of clarity in chaos. It didn't solve everything, but it planted a seed, an idea that would change how I saw everything.

***

I often dreamed of the crying mother. In some dreams, she appeared as she had on the day we first met, her face etched with desperation. Other times, she lay lifeless on a dusty road, a silent victim of the world's cruelty. But there was one dream that came more frequently, one that haunted me like no other.

In this dream, she stood on the bank of a wild, rushing river, clutching her baby to her chest as the earth beneath her feet crumbled away. The mud slid in chunks, the ground itself betraying her. Her eyes locked onto mine, wide and pleading, as I screamed and waved my arms, running toward her, desperate to reach her before it was too late. But no matter how hard I ran, the distance between us stretched impossibly long, as if the earth conspired to keep me from her.

I watched in helpless horror as the riverbank gave way entirely. She lost her footing, slipping backward, one arm flailing in the air. Her grip on the baby loosened in that split second, and the infant tumbled from her arms.

"No!" I screamed, my voice cracking as I surged forward. But it was as though I was running in place, never closing the gap. The baby hit the muddy ground, rolling down the embankment, the blanket unraveling, revealing its tiny, fragile body. The current swept it up mercilessly, pulling it downstream where it disappeared into the churning waters.

The mother's screams echoed along the river, a sound that pierced the air long after her child had vanished. But no amount of crying could bring the baby back. I stopped running, my chest heaving with breath, realizing I hadn't moved an inch closer to her.

Then, to my horror, more mothers appeared downstream, each clutching a child, their feet slipping in the same treacherous mud. One by one, they fell, their babies torn from their arms, swallowed by the relentless river. The wind howled with their cries, mingling with the roar of the water, and I stood frozen, helpless to stop any of it. I wanted to dive into the river, to rescue just one—maybe two—but I knew deep down it was futile. I couldn't save them all.

I turned and saw a group gathered on a hill under the shade of a tree, standing just above the chaos. They sang softly, their voices blending into a peaceful hymn, seemingly oblivious to the horror below them. Some glanced toward the river, their eyes briefly acknowledging the tragedy, before they turned away, retreating into their worship.

How could they turn their backs? I thought. Tears stung my eyes. We could save so many if they all just came down and jumped in. Together, we could make a difference.

I sank to the grass, head in hands, overwhelmed by the helplessness and cruel indifference of it all. Why was I, who wanted so desperately to help, stuck here, unable to even reach the riverbank, while those who could have made a difference simply sang and looked away?

A young man, whom I came to know was Jesus, broke free from the group when it seemed like all was lost. Without hesitation, he sprinted to the river, plunging into the frigid water, the current pulling at him savagely. But he swam against it, battling upstream with powerful strokes. Clinging to rocks along the way, he made his way toward the mothers, and when he reached them, he began pulling babies from the water—one by one. He cradled them, tenderly nestling them into a small shoal, safe from the raging river. He had gone upstream, where the trouble began, helping the babies before they were lost to the current.

As I watched him, I understood. It wasn't about waiting until the river was full of drowning souls but reaching them before they reached the rapids.

Dripping wet, the young man climbed out of the river, his arms full of the precious lives he saved. One by one, he returned the babies to their frantic mothers. Upstream, other mothers took notice, pausing at the river's edge, drawn by the sight of his courage. They lingered just long enough for him—and for other mothers who had already been saved—to reach them, to talk them away from the danger. Their voices carried on the wind, rippling through the chaos, until the current no longer claimed anyone else.

I wept with relief, overwhelmed by what I had witnessed. Without that man's intervention, those mothers would have lost everything.

The babies would have been swept away and families torn apart in an instant. But he had changed everything by reaching them before the tragedy. He had gone to where the crisis began, where the river was still manageable, and through his courage, he had turned what had been a river of death into a river of hope.

The answer I searched for finally became clear. I didn't need to wait for families to fall apart before stepping in. I needed to swim upstream, to where the crisis began, before the waters of extreme poverty swept children away. If I could reach them in time, I could prevent more loss and keep families intact before the current of despair tore them apart.

"Orphans are often the result of broken families, families that have been overwhelmed by circumstances beyond their control," I explained to Ben the morning after I had the dream, eager to share the revelation that had taken hold of me. "Street kids fall into prostitution or become victims of sex trafficking, their tragic circumstances pulling them under like an unstoppable current. And for years, like everyone else, I've been focused on rescuing the few orphans already swept downstream. Adoption, as noble as it is, has become the solution for the children who have fallen into the river. But it's not enough. No amount of prayers, tears, adoptive parents, or emergency aid can stop a crisis so vast. The number of orphans only grows farther downriver."

I paused, feeling the weight of the truth I uncovered. "But what if we can turn that river of death into a river of hope by going upriver, where the waters are calmer—before the tragedy strikes? What if we intervene before families break apart and the desperation becomes irreversible?"

Ben nodded slowly, the gravity of the idea settling between us. He grinned. "Yes! We must stop letting the size of the problem downstream and what everybody else says is impossible prevent us from exploring new ideas and solutions. I'm with you. But the problem upriver is pretty big, too. What do you propose we do to make an impact there?"

"I don't know yet, but I keep thinking of Isaiah 43:2, 'When you pass through the waters, I will be with you, and when you pass through the rivers, they will not sweep over you,' and I know we won't walk alone."

This was the work I had been called to do, the path I had to follow to make a difference.

But how?

***

For the first time since returning from Ethiopia, I felt a genuine surge of hope, something I hadn't experienced in months. I met with mission leaders Ben connected me with, eager to share the revelation that struck me deeply.

"International adoptions and orphan care are your focus right now," I began, choosing my words carefully. "We do what we can with the flood of orphans. But it's like jumping into a raging river—pulling as many children as possible to safety, offering them life-saving aid—only to hear more cries for help as new faces are swept into the current. We return to those waters over and over, saving the few we can while watching countless others drown." I paused, drawing in a deep breath, hoping the gravity of my words would sink in. "But why isn't anyone looking upstream? Why aren't we trying to stop these kids from becoming orphans in the first place? We need to develop a new approach that focuses on preserving vulnerable families. If catastrophic poverty is tearing apart families, then that's where our efforts must go. We must prevent orphans by tackling the root cause, poverty."

One of the board members leaned forward, echoing Ben's earlier question. "How do you propose to do that?"

I hesitated. I had ideas—glimpses of a plan—but nothing concrete yet. "I don't know exactly," I admitted. "But with funding, I'll work closely with Abebe and Abonesh in Ethiopia. They agree that orphan prevention is the missing link we need to explore, even as we continue with adoption and orphan care."

As I unfolded my vision, I watched their faces light up. The idea resonated as a solution and a shift in thinking. Together, we explored how to make the vision a reality.

To my relief, the mission leadership gave their approval. We set in motion a new initiative: Mission 1:27, inspired by the words of James: "Religion that is pure and undefiled before God the Father is this: to visit orphans and widows in their affliction..."

Over the next several weeks, I spent countless hours talking with our leadership team and close friends, brainstorming ways to intervene before desperate families disintegrated. The challenges were greater than anticipated, and time was not on our side. Most families living in extreme poverty are headed by young mothers with multiple children, abandoned by husbands who can no longer bear the burden of responsibility. These mothers, left with no options, often turned to the streets or sought out orphanages, most of which were already full.

"Imposing American solutions on an Ethiopian crisis feels wrong," I confessed to Ben one day, growing frustrated at the lack of progress. "I need to be on the ground, working with Abebe and Abonesh in person, listening to the people we aim to help. The solutions won't come from here; they must come from there. I need to see it for myself."

And so, once again, I prepared to return to Africa, this time with a new determination—not just to save the children swept downstream but to find a way to keep them and their families from ever reaching the river's edge.

Chapter Six

The Course Unknown

Familiar faces welcomed me at the airport. By now, Abebe and Abonesh were more than just colleagues. They were good friends, with us through every step of Joshua's and Aliyah's adoption and a few years later when we adopted Angelie, our ninth child. As we embraced, I felt a renewed sense of purpose. I was eager to hear their thoughts and lean on their insight as we prepared to shape the new program together. Their wisdom would be vital to turning this vision into something tangible.

"You'll be instrumental in developing these programs and figuring out how to implement them for Ethiopia's most vulnerable families using our program funds," I said the next day at breakfast.

Abebe beamed, nodding eagerly. "Then, we'll want to start where they are most desperate for help. Korah and a remote region called Dembidolo, about 375 miles west of Addis Abba, near the Sudan Border."

"I like a good road trip!" I said as if this was anything like the trips I'd taken before, trying not to worry. I had a tough time in Korah before and heard terrifying tales of the dangers of venturing too far into the wilds of Ethiopia. I was nervous with so much at stake and so many depending on our success.

"Then you'll love this." Abonesh grinned, catching Abebe's eye.

They laughed. Two days and almost twenty-four hours of torturous driving later, I understood why.

Abebe and I jumped in a van before dawn the next day to avoid traffic and get a jump on the trip. We quickly climbed in elevation with the capital city in our rearview mirror. The roads curled through mountainous terrain, revealing exotic beauty and stunning vistas with every switchback. It didn't take long before it felt like we were in the middle of nowhere. Strangely, Ethiopia's blue lakes and heavily treed valleys reminded me of Minnesota's Lake Minnetonka, where I fished with my dad as a boy. Thoughts of America quickly faded when I spotted baboons staring at me from the trees and hippos rising from the water. When we headed out of the hills and into the bush country and wilderness, I took it all in like I was visiting Africa for the first time. Everything was so different from my previous experiences. The air seemed fresher, my mind clearer. Despite my initial trepidation over venturing so far from the familiar, seeing more remote areas of Ethiopia excited me. I took it all in with a renewed sense of wonder.

We passed little grass huts and women carrying water jugs on their heads and babies on their hips. Children played everywhere, and little boys and older men shepherded flocks of sheep and herds of dusty cattle. Here and there, men plowed rich-looking fields with oxen. In scarce towns, people sat in groups on the ground, laughing, talking, and playing simple games. Though people were poor in these places, they were making lives for themselves. Though poor and struggling to meet daily needs, most people here had enough to survive. They appeared carefree, without what many people needed to live happy lives in America. They lived simple, peaceful lives, low to the ground, one with the earth.

I envied their simple lives and purity of spirit. I thought about what I needed to be happy and content, wondering if it was far less than I realized and reflecting again on the sheer amount of stuff I had.

As we drove deeper into the countryside, Abebe and I discussed the new orphan prevention program. The conversation flowed quicker and more naturally than it ever could over phone calls or emails, and we accomplished more in those few hours than I'd hoped. Abebe had an intimate understanding of the people living in crippling poverty. His mind brimmed with ideas. A brilliant man with years of ministry experience, he knew how to navigate the complexities of working with the government, but his heart was massive—full of compassion for widows, orphans, and the destitute. His passion for improving their lives fueled every suggestion he made. Open-minded and eager to explore new approaches, Abebe was an essential partner in shaping Mission 1:27 from the very beginning.

The road worsened the deeper into the country we drove, sometimes becoming nothing more than ruts in the packed dirt or faint, muddy tracks. Though few signs marked the way, our driver knew where he was going, and we made steady progress. We slowed and stopped frequently, avoiding livestock and other hazards. Sheep, goats, cattle, and people shared the roads with cars and vans in a free-for-all, even in small, isolated villages where people wore surprised and curious faces as we rolled by. Crowds gathered to peer in the windows if we stopped the van for any time. Most people smiled, obviously curious and friendly. But this was not always the case.

In one village, men sat on the side of the road, casually holding AK-47s. "They could be part of the Federal Police, Army, or some tribal militia," Abebe said.

Whoever they were, they didn't make me feel comfortable or safe.

We brought food to sustain us during our journey and avoided stopping in hostile villages. "It's safe for the most part, but caution is always best. We don't want to draw attention to ourselves, especially with you being American," Abebe said. "You are not always popular here."

Danger could strike anytime here. Many in the region are Muslim extremists, making travel especially dangerous for Westerners. Kidnappings and killings are not unusual.

We drove through the night while I fitfully drifted off to sleep, waking when we hit a massive pothole, and the van frame slammed into hard-packed gravel with a solid thud. Just as I dozed off again, the driver slammed the brakes to avoid plowing into a group of people and animals crossing the road.

Hours passed. The sun peered over a distant mountain range when we stopped for a quick bathroom break along the side of the road and then continued our journey down the mud-slogged thoroughfare on an arduous journey I worried might never end.

"The area had significant rainfall the last few nights. It'll be better when we get into the hills again," Abebe said.

I admired his confidence, but it did us no good when we descended a treacherously steep hill, slipping and sliding until mud gave way beneath us in a heady rush. We rode the mudslide to the bottom, only to face a steep hill ahead.

Our back wheels slid and tried to grip but only spun, sending flecks of mud flying. Before our driver could do anything to stop it, we skidded sideways into a ditch, tottering enough to make me think we'd go over on our side before the van righted itself and came to a stop, tires buried in mud, a few feet from where a large crew had stopped work on the now impassable road. We were stuck.

"Should we get out and push?" I asked, doubting we could call AAA.

The roadworkers stared and chatted with one another, looking intrigued by our predicament. Most stayed where they were, but a few walked toward the van.

We'd intended to move quickly, staying under the radar. As long as we kept moving, we were safe. The last thing I wanted was to be stuck and unable to escape, surrounded by people with guns and very much on the radar.

"Go in the back. Draw the curtains," Abebe said tensely in a tone I'd never heard him use before.

I quickly hid in the back of the van as the crew boss appeared.

The Ethiopian government was building new roads, so the crew of men was not unusual, but their Chinese boss, who came marching down the hill, took me by surprise. Yelling angry commands, the Ethiopian workers either ignored or didn't understand, he looked out of place in his fancy Western clothing and shiny boots. I gathered that he was angry that we had prevented his road crew from proceeding with their work.

I lay flat on the dusty floor of the van as angry voices rose, and I wondered if I would see my family again. *How did I end up here?*

A few years ago, I couldn't have imagined traveling to such a remote and hostile part of Ethiopia, the only Westerner for hundreds of miles, far from help of any kind, vulnerable and uncertain, so far from my American comfort zone.

The crew finally understood their Chinese commander's instructions and gathered around the van, pushing together. The van rocked back and forth, axles squealing.

I kept out of sight as we gained traction and got underway again after what seemed like hours of heart-stopping danger. Our driver pulled over a mile or so down the road so I could climb back into the passenger seat, relieved the ordeal was over.

After two long and rough days of driving day and night, we arrived in Dembidolo, a place that must hold the world record for the most enormous potholes. Although more rural and remote than Korah, the poverty was similar. Abebe said they were so remote that no one aided them except the local pastor, who did what he could with the small funds the church sent him.

Dembidolo lay nestled in the heart of Ethiopia's lush highlands, where time seemed to stretch and fold into itself, untouched by the modern rush of the outside world. The road leading into town was a winding ribbon of red earth, flanked on either side by towering eucalyptus trees that whispered in the breeze, their scent mingling with the rich, fertile soil. The sun hung low in the sky, casting a warm golden light over the landscape, its rays topping the hills like a veil as it set.

The town was a patchwork of tiny homes and market stalls, each worn by the hands of time but alive with color and the hum of life. Tin roofs glinted atop walls of mud and clay, their rough textures a testament to resilience. Children played barefoot in the narrow streets, their laughter mingling with the soft bleating of goats and the calls of women selling fresh produce from woven baskets. Everything here was slower, deliberate, as though the land breathed with gentle patience.

But there was an undercurrent in Dembidolo that was impossible to ignore. Behind the beauty of the rolling hills and the bustling market, there was an unspoken weight—an invisible thread connecting every family and face to the harsh realities of life in this remote town. The people lived on the edge, their livelihoods dictated by the whims of the land and the scarcity that haunted even the most fertile soil. Yet, in the quiet moments, beneath the surface, there was a deep resilience, a strength that came from knowing survival here was both an art and a necessity.

Smoke from cooking fires spiraled into the sky, curling like whispers from the homes scattered across the countryside. Dembidolo was suspended between beauty and hardship, where hope flickered like a candle in the wind—fragile but never extinguished.

Pastor Garamu and a young man named Wakjira met and warmly greeted us. Short and round, Garamu had a deep voice and robust laugh. He oversaw 270 regional churches and was respected by everybody who knew him, according to Abebe. I could see why, liking him right away.

Wakjira grew up as an orphan in Dembidollo. When we met, he was in his late twenties, gentle, and soft-spoken. As the director of the mission's orphanage in Dembidollo, he was familiar with the impoverished families and eager to help us explore new ways to help people here.

"The good pastor and Wakjira will connect us with the key people in Dembidolo," Abebe promised.

Pastor Garamu took us to our hotel, a place unlike any hotel I'd seen in America. The building codes and quality control were very different in this part of the world. The whole place glowed with dim lights, and the steps to the second floor were not the same height, which made climbing them with my large suitcase a near-death experience. Relieved to find a bathroom with a toilet in my room, I didn't know how to sit on it since the front of the toilet bowl was only one inch from the wall. Nothing in the room was straight, level, or even, and the faucet handle fell off when I tried to wash my hands. That didn't matter, I learned, turning the other handle and getting no running water. To make matters worse, I was not alone in my room. Cockroaches crawled everywhere, unspooked by me or the light.

Exhausted and unsure of how I'd ever go to sleep, I crawled into a tiny, uncomfortable bed and covered myself with a ragged blanket. All I could think about was the cockroaches until I thought about how far away I was from the comforts of home. Thankfully, I surprised myself and fell asleep, my heart sad and overwhelmed.

After some sleep, the next day seemed brighter, and I was grateful to leave my room and meet Abebe, Pastor Garamu, and Wakjira. Outside, I got my first view of Dembidolo in bright daylight. It looked like a war zone, with streets full of massive potholes, no cement or asphalt, and many of the buildings in shambles.

People stopped and stared as if they saw a ghost when I walked by.

"It has been quite a while since a white person was here. Very few white people have even been here," Abebe explained when a child cried and ran back to a group of mothers who stared at me.

When we stopped for any time, a crowd gathered. Sometimes, this made it hard to get around or uncomfortable, with hands grabbing at me and people pressing close in a way that took getting used to. Americans have the luxury of personal space they do not have in many parts of the world.

Uncomfortable, no longer incognito, and the talk of the town, I worried until Pastor Garamu assured me everything would be good and promised to stay with us. It helped ease my nervousness when the townspeople, obviously respecting him, paid their respects as we passed.

Over the next few days, we visited several of Dembidolo's most impoverished families.

"Many women here are desperate. Some are alone. They took their children to another village or town to work because they couldn't feed them, starving themselves. Many have not seen their children in years and have no idea how they are doing. Many have given up, just waiting to die. If not for the kindness of others, many would be dead already," Wakjira said. "They are as poor as any people I had ever seen, suffering a level of hopelessness and desperation beyond words."

I could not pick one of my children to sacrifice, to take to another city and leave on the street, hoping they would make it, walking away from them forever. I don't think many Americans could imagine such a terrible thing.

"So many broken families and broken lives. Poverty is an evil and heartless monster that destroys people and families, crushing them physically, emotionally, mentally, and socially," the pastor said.

We talked with several women who still had their children, asking questions about what they had, what they wanted, and what would help them feed their children so their families could stay together.

"We want families to thrive, not just survive," I said, Garamu acting as translator.

The women seemed excited, if somewhat skeptical. Few women in this situation managed such a feat, and they felt lucky to eat every few days. Supporting themselves and their children seemed impossible to most.

Despite the utter poverty, the way of life there was also incredibly beautiful and simple. Friendly and welcoming people opened the doors to their little huts and shared their lives, hopes, and dreams for their families.

Though I often felt out of place in this unfamiliar land, I gave thanks more and more as God's purpose for my time here began to unfold. Immersing myself in the poverty-stricken communities brought a clarity I hadn't experienced during my earlier trips to Ethiopia. Spending time with the people—listening to their stories, sharing meals, witnessing their daily struggles—shaped my understanding in ways that mere observation never could. Their warmth and kindness softened the challenges of navigating a culture so different from my own. I had come here with plans, but it wasn't until I lived among them that I saw how deeply they needed to change.

As Abebe and I met with various families, we began to see the bigger picture, and the pieces slowly started to fall into place. One afternoon, we visited a small group of women who turned their homes into makeshift workshops, weaving blankets by hand to sell in the local markets. The blankets were modest but beautiful, and their generated income helped these women feed their families. One woman, her face etched with years of hardship, gave us a stack of freshly woven blankets to take back to the orphans. "These will keep the children warm this winter," she said softly, pride evident in her voice. It struck me then—these women weren't just surviving; they were supporting others, lifting others as they lifted themselves.

As we left the workshop, the idea came to me like a spark. "What if this could be the answer?" I said, turning to Abebe as we walked along a narrow dirt road. "What if we could help more families start small businesses like this?"

Abebe nodded thoughtfully, the wheels visibly turning in his mind. "Many families could benefit from something like this. It doesn't have to be much—a little capital, just enough to get them started, could make all the difference. A simple business could help a family stay together and, more importantly, keep their children out of orphanages."

We spent the next few days talking with local families, listening to their dreams and struggles. One young couple wanted to open a small vegetable stand in the market but lacked the money to buy seeds. Another man hoped to start a bicycle repair shop to help his village, where transportation was a lifeline. Every conversation revealed another possibility.

Inspired by the women who weave blankets, we recognized this as a model for empowering families to rise out of poverty. By the time we finished our visit, we had identified several families to include in a pilot program. The plan was simple yet powerful. Pastor Garamu and Abebe would collaborate closely with each family to identify small, sustainable businesses that could be started with minimal seed money. Whether it involved weaving blankets, selling produce, or repairing bicycles, we aimed to provide parents with the means to support themselves and keep their families together.

As we waved goodbye to our new friends in Dembidolo, I felt alive with renewed purpose. "This could really work, Abebe," I said, my voice hopeful.

Returning to Addis Ababa, our conversations were full of excitement and possibility. We discussed the logistics—how to get the initial funds, scale the program, and ensure the families received ongoing support. There were potential problems, too, of course. Would the businesses be sustainable? Would the families stick with it if times got tough? But for every doubt, there was hope that this fledgling program could change lives and be a path to something more lasting than emergency aid or temporary fixes.

I couldn't help but feel that this idea of preventing orphans by strengthening families—was the answer I had been seeking all along.

A few days later, as I settled into my seat for the long flight home, a sense of clarity formed—but it wasn't without the shadow of familiar fears creeping in. The vision was clear as day. We would step in before families crumbled and children became orphans and give them the tools to survive. But as the enormity of the task settled over me, I felt a familiar tightness in my chest. That same old feeling—of not being enough and failing before I even began—rose like a tide I thought I'd long since escaped.

The doubts I buried, the ones I never quite confronted, surfaced. How would I manage this massive undertaking? What if I wasn't equipped for what lay ahead? Fear gripped me as it had in the darkest moments of my life. I remembered the years when fear and hopelessness ruled me when I was sure I would never amount to anything. It was only when I turned to Jesus, when I finally let go, that I found the strength to rise above my crippling doubts. My faith became the anchor that steadied me in the storm of fear.

As the plane climbed higher and I struggled to leave worries behind me, with home in sight, I needed that strength again. Only the same surrender and faith that saved me before could see me through this daunting journey. I closed my eyes, letting memories wash over me.

Chapter Seven

Waters Rising

Fear subtly influenced my life, creeping like a shadow at the fringes of my consciousness, roots deeply planted after a terrifying incident during a family fishing trip to Lake Minnetonka, Minnesota, where I nearly drowned. My dad yanked me from the abyss that day, but part of me remained submerged, trapped in those moments of panic. After the incident, as the years passed, my fear transformed into a pervasive sense of dread, tightening its hold on me like a vise, especially throughout my tumultuous teenage years, becoming a constant, unpredictable presence. Anxiety attacks stripped away my self-confidence, leaving me ashamed and fearful.

I kept my struggle hidden, hoping no one would notice. I was longing for relief but did not know where to find it.

At sixteen, I turned to alcohol, a temporary escape leading me further into destructive habits. I drank as often as I could, hoping for a reprieve, but liquor pushed me deeper into behaviors I'd once feared—sometimes, I even became the bully I despised. On the outside, I seemed tough, a person you wouldn't want to mess with. But that image was nothing more than a mask to cover up my fear.

After high school, I signed up for the Air Force's delayed entry program. Chris and I were together, dreaming of the future. It was supposed to be a time of excitement and new beginnings. But everything changed one summer day while riding motorcycles with a friend. My engine caught fire. I tried to put it out alone on the trail, but the gas tank exploded, and flames engulfed me. The pain was excruciating as my skin burned, and I was helpless to stop it. My friend circled back, found me, and extinguished the flames. The ride to the hospital felt endless, every moment filled with agony.

Chris supported me through every challenge, taking care of me when I couldn't manage on my own. What should have been a time of embracing adulthood turned into a struggle marked by pain and dependence on her. I always wanted to be the strong one. Yet, circumstances forced me to lean on her in ways I hadn't anticipated, placing an unintended burden on her that I deeply regretted.

The accident led to a medical discharge from the Air Force. My plans unraveled, and after several months of recovery and no plan B, I enlisted in the Army. It seemed like the only path left that could provide a stable future for Chris and me now that we were engaged.

As our first year of marriage and my time in the Army whirled by like the changing seasons, I found myself anticipating the arrival of our first child while preparing for a new chapter in Ft. Lewis, Washington. Despite the excitement surrounding us, an unsettling emptiness lingered within me, a void I couldn't quite comprehend. I felt adrift, lost in a sea of emotions, unable to articulate what was wrong or why peace seemed perpetually out of reach. I sensed something significant was missing from our lives—an elusive puzzle piece we couldn't quite name or grasp.

During many sleepless nights, my thoughts turned to the church I attended as a boy, a place in my childhood that always felt safe, where I was happy and close to God. I remembered how the bible stories stirred a comfortable feeling in me, even if I hadn't let them take root then. As an adult, I believed in God, sure, but that belief grew distant as I aged, like a fading memory tucked away in my mind and heart, not a belief that guided me or shaped my life. But with fatherhood looming and fear pressing in from every side, I knew I couldn't carry this alone any longer. Something had to change. I had to find help. Desperate, I turned to the church.

Chris and I found a small Christian church near our new home. The building was modest, the congregation even smaller, but the moment we stepped inside, they embraced us as if we had always belonged. We were the youngest ones there, but it didn't matter. They welcomed us with open arms, their warmth cutting through the fog of fear that had settled over me. In their acceptance, I found the relief and support I longed for.

Slowly, something shifted. The sermons started hitting differently, as if each word and scripture were crafted just for me. They were not just stories anymore; they were truths I needed to hear. The messages of love, peace, and forgiveness stirred something inside me, like a light flickering in a dark room, casting shadows into areas I ignored for too long. My faith was not just a belief but a transformative force that changed my perspective and gave me the courage to confront my fears.

Then came the dreams. The first one was so vivid that I woke drenched in sweat, my heart pounding. The sky darkened in the dream, clouds swirling in a fevered dance as thunder rumbled overhead. The air crackled with energy, and then—there He was. Jesus, descending from the heavens, bathed in a brilliant white light. In that instant, I wasn't ready for Him. I was lost and unworthy, and it felt too late to change. The fear that lived inside me was magnified and almost unbearable. When I woke, I trembled, the remnants of the dream still clinging to me.

Not long after, I had another dream of hearing a knock at my door. I opened it, and there stood Jesus, His eyes piercing yet filled with love and understanding. He didn't say a word, but His gaze spoke volumes. I woke, shaken by the encounter, unable to ignore the feeling that He was calling me to something I had been running from my entire life.

The more I heard in church, the clearer it became. The fear, the failures, the endless striving to prove myself—they were what separated me from God. I spent my life trying to control everything, carrying burdens I was never meant to carry alone. And yet, through it all, He had been there. I just hadn't realized it. I hadn't let Him in to help me.

The lights came on in my soul. For the first time, I realized what was missing and what I needed. It was not something but someone. It was Jesus. My rebellion and sin separated me from Him, though He offered forgiveness by His sacrifice on the cross. He died for me so I could be forgiven and receive eternal life. He wanted to set me free from all the guilt and shame I carried for so many years. I only needed to accept.

At the end of one Sunday service, the pastor invited us to place our trust in Jesus as Lord and Savior. "God's been waiting for you to come to Him," he said.

His words struck something deep inside me. I couldn't wait another moment and went forward, Chris closely behind me.

From that day on, everything changed. My newfound faith touched every part of my life, even areas I had long resented. The world felt different and brighter as if I had been seeing it in shades of gray before, and now, for the first time, I saw full color. I had never experienced such peace or joy. For the first time, I understood what it meant to be free.

The Army, which I once despised, became an unlikely proving ground. What I once saw as a cage—its routines, its rigid discipline—now seemed like a structure I could use to grow. Instead of counting down the days until I could leave, I leaned into the challenges with a quiet strength, a new sense that I wasn't doing this alone anymore.

It wasn't long before my outlook started to show. I enrolled in night school, something I'd never imagined myself capable of, but my newfound faith unlocked confidence I didn't know I had. In class, I found that I wasn't the person I'd always believed myself to be. I wasn't the dumb kid who couldn't keep up. I could learn. I could excel.

At work, the change was even more apparent. My superiors took notice, encouraging me to compete in soldier competitions, something I would have never dreamed of doing before. I hesitated at first. Old doubts and fears tried to creep back in, whispering that I wasn't good enough and would fail. But then, I remembered I wasn't carrying those old weights anymore. And so, I competed. To my amazement, I won—first the title of Best Soldier in my Company, then in the Battalion, and eventually in the Brigade. Before I knew it, I competed for Fort Lewis's Soldier of the Year.

Every success stripped another layer of old fear away. The talents and strengths buried under years of self-doubt and guilt began to surface like treasures hidden for far too long. I began to see myself as God saw me—capable, valuable, with purpose.

Still, even with this growing confidence, sometimes old fears tried to return. The fear of not being enough and failure were familiar, like old wounds that hadn't fully healed. I still struggled at times with gripping fear and panic attacks, though my newfound faith equipped me to better combat my familiar demons.

Many years later, looking back at those long-ago days, facing the monumental task of preventing children from becoming orphans, those fears crept back in. The weight of the work ahead felt daunting, even overwhelming. The scope of saving children before they were lost to poverty, abandonment, and despair was greater than anything I'd faced. What if I wasn't enough? What if I failed, not just myself but the families and children depending on me now? People I'd made promises to?

The journey ahead was long, with many challenges, but faith isn't a one-time act. It's a daily surrender, a daily choice to trust that God will carry me through as He has before. And just as I knew He pulled me from the waters of Lake Minnetonka all those years ago, I knew God would pull me through this.

The mission I was about to undertake was bigger than me and more significant than me. It wasn't about me. It was about surrendering to God's path, knowing He would guide my steps, even when I couldn't see the way ahead. With faith and fear mingling in my chest, I entered the unknown, trusting that God would carry me through again.

***

The program's early days were a blur of hope, uncertainty, and determination. What started as a vision, something born out of a restless urgency to intervene before families fell apart, took shape. We spent the first few months building relationships with local leaders, identifying needy families, and developing the small business models that would hopefully sustain them. Every decision felt monumental.

Abebe and I spent long hours in the field, visiting homes and talking to mothers already pushed to the brink of despair, their eyes hollow from the weight of uncertainty. Their husbands had abandoned some, leaving them to raise children on their own with nothing but scraps of hope to cling to. They teetered on the edge of poverty, knowing one misstep could send their families spiraling into ruin. Each conversation reinforced the urgency of what we were trying to do.

We started small, just a handful of families at first. Pastor Garamu worked closely with them, helping them establish small businesses—selling produce, weaving blankets, repairing bicycles—anything that could give them a foothold in a life that felt increasingly precarious. The idea was simple yet profound. If we could help families sustain themselves, we could prevent the collapse that claimed so many others.

As word spread of our new program, something remarkable happened. More families came forward, desperate for the chance to stabilize their lives. The need was staggering, but so was the response. We expected slow, steady growth, maybe a few dozen families in the first year—but before we knew it, the program swelled beyond our wildest expectations. One day, as Abebe and I reviewed the latest reports, the numbers hit me: 150 families had enrolled in the program.

It felt surreal like we had somehow stepped into a larger narrative than we imagined. These were no longer just numbers on a page—these were families, lives intertwined with ours, all waiting to see if this lifeline would hold. Only a few weeks in, and the success of these first families would determine everything. It wasn't just about them; it was about the program's future. Could it scale? Could we find the funding to support even more families? Would we still be smiling in six months? A year?

The pressure weighed heavily on me, old fears whispering that I wasn't enough to carry this. But alongside those fears, there was something else, a deep, quiet hope. The program had grown, not because of my strength or abilities, but because this was the work God set before us. He brought us this far, and we must trust Him to carry us further, I decided.

And so, we waited—watching, hoping, praying—to see how these families would fare. The results would be the proof we needed to justify expanding our efforts, proving we could intervene before it was too late. It was a delicate, uncertain time, yet I held tightly to quiet resolve.

***

A year passed. What began as a fragile idea grew into something substantial despite a challenging journey filled with sleepless nights and endless planning. Each small victory propelled us forward, driven by a purpose greater than ourselves, lighting our path in the dark.

Our mission expanded, stretching from the heart of Korah to the distant hills of Dembidolo. What began as a small initiative touched the lives of 150 families, each a testament to the power of hope and the strength of community. Every family brought a unique story, and as our program grew, so did the profound realization that this work would do much more than provide a temporary fix. We allowed people to build something lasting, alleviating poverty, empowering lives, and strengthening the foundations of families on the brink of collapse.

The more we pushed forward, the more the essence of our mission revealed itself. This was about more than funds, numbers, or reports—it was about the faces of those we were helping, the mothers who could now feed their children, and the fathers who found dignity in work. It was about the children who would grow up with the possibility of something more than mere survival. Each new connection, each family added to the program, made the weight of our responsibility more tangible, more real.

Fundraising became my constant companion. I traveled from church to church, from conference to conference, speaking to anyone who would listen about the devastating poverty in Ethiopia. I told them about Korah, the mothers who couldn't afford a meal for their children, and the hopelessness that clung to people's faces like a second skin. I told them about Dembidolo, where the land was fertile, but the people were trapped in cycles of poverty that seemed impossible to break. And when I spoke about our work and showed pictures Abebe sent of families we'd saved, something shifted in the room. People wanted to get involved—not because of grand gestures, but because they realized how little it took to change lives. A few dollars could feed a family. A small investment could start a business. These weren't abstract ideas but tangible realities, and people responded with open hearts.

Abebe and Abonesh became the steady hands guiding the program in Ethiopia, and their leadership was invaluable. Every month, I looked forward to their reports and updates about families finding their footing and children who no longer went to bed hungry. Each call reassured me that what we were doing was making a real difference. The stories filled me with anticipation—I couldn't wait to return and see it all for myself, to stand where lives were being transformed.

This time, I wasn't going alone. A colleague from work, Ethan Bauer, had agreed to accompany me after hearing me speak about the mission enough times to feel compelled to see it firsthand. Together, we would witness what had been built over the last year. I was eager to show him the heart of the work we poured so much into.

We'd become close after he cornered me at a national sales meeting and asked how I managed to do everything, including pastoring, adopting, managing a large family, working at a demanding sales job, and running an aid effort in Africa simultaneously.

His question took me aback. "I don't think about it. I just do it," I said. "My priorities are God, my wife, family, job, and health. I don't have time for it if it doesn't fall into one of those priorities."

As our friendship deepened, we discussed my work in Ethiopia with the orphan prevention program.

"Let me know when you set up the next trip," Ethan said.

When I did, he said there was no reason he shouldn't come. "What are we going to do to help?" he asked after he confirmed his reservation. I learned right away that Ethan is full of questions.

"God asked me that in Korah, which started me on this journey. And I'm still asking it. It's hard to give you a clear answer," I said. "We'll have scheduled visits, follow-ups with our sponsored families for progress reports and the like, but the rest...well, we go where God takes us. I've helped with some building projects in Ethiopia, but Ethiopians tell me they don't need help fixing or building things. They want a relationship. The fact that we come to be with them is enough." I hoped I hadn't deterred him. Americans always want to do something when they go to a foreign country to offer help. We want to build or fix things, to create something. We want to take pictures of what we did to show people back home.

Someone once asked me, "What gives you the right to go there and tell these people how to live or fix their problems? That's just American arrogance in action. It's better to leave them alone. Let them handle it. Survival of the fittest." At first, I was furious. How could someone be so cold, so blind to the struggles of the poor? To suggest such a thing felt heartless. However, as time went on, and after countless conversations with people in Ethiopia, I began to understand what he meant. He wasn't entirely wrong. It wasn't about swooping in with ready-made solutions; it was about listening, learning, and working with the people, not for them, to help find a way forward that respected their culture and realities.

"The spirit of the Ethiopian people moved me to try and help them after my first trip. And to keep myself open to what they can teach me if I listen without trying to fix everything." I grinned. "You'll see," I told him on the plane heading to Africa. "By the end of our trip, you will know what to do."

Chapter Eight

Waters Parting, Dreams Renewed

The journey had been long and challenging, and in many ways, we were still just starting. We built something significant, planting seeds of hope along the way. Now, I was ready to see the results.

Ethan was determined to understand every aspect of our work with families. His questions were relentless, and often, I didn't have clear answers. He pushed me to dig deeper, reexamine our approach, and explore ideas we'd never considered. Incredibly sharp, he learned quickly and produced solutions on the spot, things no one had thought of before. Within a day, my mind was buzzing with new possibilities. I found myself hoping Ethan would be convinced to join the mission by the end of the trip.

We didn't ease into the experience; instead, we dove straight into the heart of it. We spent our first day in Korah, the leper colony built around a garbage dump, visiting families I knew from my first trip. I wanted Ethan to see what I had seen and hear his thoughts.

We visited an older man, his body destroyed by years of leprosy. In a dark room, he lay on an old mat on the floor. The ceiling was open in places, and the mud roof was failing. Cobwebs and dust decorated every corner. The man, his face sunken, cheekbones sharp, had no nose, only a gaping hole where it should have been. His hands were clubs with no fingers. He suffered unbelievably, yet he was kind and smiling like many old and needy people in Korah.

Abebe talked to him briefly before I sat on the edge of the bed and held his hand.

The leper spoke softly, and Abebe translated. "He says he is just waiting to die, and his only wish is to see the face of Jesus. He is at peace, he says."

When we left, Ethan stopped me a few paces from the hut, wiping watery eyes. "He wanted nothing material. Not even the ability to walk again. What are we doing?" He sighed loudly. "Back home, I mean. What are our priorities, wants, and needs? I cannot cross the distance in our experiences. These people have nothing, yet they have more faith than anyone I've ever known. They ask for nothing." His voice broke.

"It's a whole new perspective," I said, knowing the feelings gripping him and how hard it was to reconcile the conditions in the slum with our abundance. "People here come out of falling down shacks, bent over, and with nothing, yet they greet us warmly. They are so happy. It breaks you up even more."

From that moment, Ethan was all in. "It seems like so much of what people think they need to do to help people here comes from an American perspective. We try to get them to a place like ours, which feels impossible. But people don't need that much."

"You're right. Making them more like us isn't going to happen, but we can free them from poverty so they can sustain themselves, feed their kids, and send them to school," I said. "It takes almost nothing to start a business and save lives. I've seen even a bit of help give someone life-changing hope."

"Their lives will never look like ours, so that shouldn't be our goal." Ethan chewed on the problem. I could practically see the wheels turning as he thought of ways to improve the program. Ethan saw the desperation up close—families scavenging for survival, children growing up in conditions that seemed impossible to endure—and he wanted to fix it all. More than once, tears filled his eyes as the magnitude of the problems hit him.

"It's overwhelming, isn't it?" I said gently after a particularly rough house visit. "It never gets easier to see. But there's hope here, too. You'll understand when we meet some of the people in the program. As bad as it is, miracles happen here every day."

I told him about a street beggar who affected me heavily in the early days of my work. At the very bottom of the bottom, she'd been raped, beaten, and left for dead. Surviving, she found she was pregnant and gave birth in the tiniest of rooms at a friend's hut, lucky to have anyone to save her from having her baby in the street like an animal. When I crouched down in the tiny makeshift hut this poor woman and her new baby called home, I found a place unfit for humans to live in. She couldn't feed herself, let alone nurse her new baby, unable to produce milk because she was starving to death. As I knelt before her, I wept uncontrollably. *If you walk out of here and leave her like that, you are not a Christian.*

"I thought of a quote from the Book of James—'What good is it, my brothers, if someone says he has faith but does not have works? Can that faith save him? If a brother or sister is poorly clothed and lacking in daily food, and one of you says to them, 'Go in peace, be warmed and filled,' without giving them the things needed for the body, what good is that?' and I understood faith by itself, if it does not have works, is nothing," I said.

Genuine faith shows itself through actions.

"Crying in that poor mother's hut, everything we'd built—the mission, the programs, the systems—became painfully personal," I told Ethan, my voice heavy with the memory. "I spent so much time in the logistics of starting the mission, in the numbers and operations, that I'd started to lose touch with the human side. I became detached from the stories of desperation that first drove me to start this work. But sitting in that hut, looking into that woman's eyes, I was reminded how real this is—how every day is a battle between life and death for these families. I realized I needed to come here more often, spend time with the people in their homes, and feel that reality regularly. It helped me understand how hard it is for people back home to imagine this kind of suffering."

I paused, catching Ethan's stricken gaze. "Before we left, we got her into the program. There was no time to wait. Helping her was literally a matter of survival."

I leaned forward, trying to make him see the connection. "This is why hope has to trump despair, Ethan. Why you have to hold it in your heart no matter what. The pain and suffering can overwhelm you if you let it, but there's always hope. That mother's life will change because of a small act because we didn't give up. And that's what you'll see in the program—miracles happen when we refuse to let the despair drown us and recognize the power in the tiniest of actions when it comes to helping people."

"I have so many questions. Why is it like this? The problems and magnitude are almost overwhelming," Ethan said as we walked through crowds of people, some barefoot, draped in rags, others in expensive, western clothes or colorful *habesha kemis* dresses made from cotton featuring intricate handwoven patterns on the hems and sleeves, and shawls, known as a *netela*. Everyone mingled with sheep, goats, donkeys, beggars, and horses in the city streets.

I sighed, taking it all in, trying to see it through Ethan's eyes. "There is no answer. What you see is what you get. Struggling to understand something so impossible is fruitless and helps no one," I said. "After a while, you'll stop asking, but you never stop caring."

"Best to focus on what we can do. The impact on the families we serve is incredible," Abebe echoed the next day, taking us into the home of a program family. "Jeff, you might recall her from your last visit. Her name is Waganesh. She had HIV and tuberculosis and was near death, so she couldn't care for her little boy. With a heavy heart, she had handed him over to her neighbor, feeling the pain of separation as she hoped they would give him the care she could no longer provide."

I remembered her. She'd been unable to walk, lying on a worn mat on the dirty floor, so sick she couldn't take the powerful HIV medications we brought her because she needed food to take it with, and she had none. When we left her the year before, I thought I would never see her again, that she would be dead in days.

"Hers was the first family in Korah we sponsored, the most in need," Abebe said when introducing her to Ethan, his eyes filling with tears and his voice shaking. "I wanted hers to be the first you see now."

She moved toward us with a grace I hardly recognized, her arms outstretched for an embrace, her face lit with a joy so pure it was almost impossible to reconcile with the woman I'd once known. Health and spirit radiated from her as if life had bloomed within her again. I stood there, stunned by the transformation before me. Had I not seen it with my eyes, I might have thought it impossible.

"Sponsorship provided Waganesh with regular milk and food so she could take her medicine. Eventually, she could bring her child back home and care for him again by making soap in molds with supplies we helped her buy. Now, she's working with other women to find better ways to bring water to more people here." Abebe beamed as the little boy ran around the small room on sturdy little legs, delighted with a tiny toy car Ethan gave him. "The little help we provided made the difference between life and death for him and his mother and others they've helped."

"She's like Lazarus, raised from the dead," our Korah case manager, Tesfaye, said.

"We saved her life, Jeff. Preserved her little family of two." Abebe gave me one of his spontaneous embraces.

"Your program prevented an orphan." Ethan's voice echoed my amazement at seeing our success for the first time in person.

Filled with encouragement, joy, and a clear purpose and calling, we visited more families in our new program, seeing over and over again how a little help produced an abundance of hope and wealth in the lives of the truly, desperately poor.

Though our parent organization remained deeply committed to caring for orphans through adoption and delivering critical relief—food, medicine, and supplies to those in immediate need, our new program marked a turning point. It offered hope where traditional aid could no longer reach, providing families a chance to survive and thrive. It was a model of sustainability that empowered families to support themselves, keep their children with them, and break the cycle of poverty. Cost-effective and replicable, it became more than just a temporary solution; it was a lifeline that gave the community the tools to rebuild from within, restoring dignity and fostering resilience in places where despair had once seemed unshakable. The change was real; you could see it in the children's laughter and their parents' confident strides, building something lasting.

The trip to Korah with Ethan was nothing like my first. Back then, I'd been overwhelmed, stumbling through a haze of shock, barely able to process the depth of the suffering I encountered. But this time was different. Walking beside Ethan, seeing the world through his fresh, unjaded eyes, something inside me shifted. It opened my heart in ways I hadn't expected, allowing me to feel our work's total weight and beauty again. It reignited something in me, something I'd nearly forgotten: the deep well of hope and humanity that can so quickly get buried beneath the endless grind of coordination and day-to-day operations that were part of a start-up relief effort.

As we left Korah, I wasn't weighed down by despair like before. Instead, I was filled with a new sense of joy, a quiet excitement that hummed through me as we set out on the long journey to Dembidolo. I wasn't just surviving the experience this time but eager for it. Eager to see the next chapter of our work unfold, eager to witness the changes our program was making, and hopeful for the possibilities ahead.

This time, we chose a better vehicle, a Land Cruiser. I wasn't about to get stuck in the mud in hostile territory again.

It was a joy to watch Ethan take in the foreign sights, sounds, and smells as we journeyed deeper into the remote regions of Ethiopia. Everything seemed new to him, the vibrant markets, the earthy scent of the countryside, the voices of the people speaking in unfamiliar rhythms. His eyes lit up with curiosity at every turn, his mind racing to absorb and understand this new world. His excitement was contagious, sparking lively conversations between him, Abebe, and me as we traveled, each bouncing ideas off the other, exploring new possibilities for our mission.

Ethan's interest in our work grew by the day. He was meticulous and process-driven, unlike me, who often relied on intuition and experience. His attention to detail and knack for structure brought a fresh perspective to our efforts. He saw connections I hadn't noticed and found efficiencies I hadn't considered. Where I saw complexity, he saw systems waiting to be refined. It was clear that his strengths filled the gaps in my own.

"You know, Ethan, your strengths could be so helpful to develop this work further," I told him.

He grinned, surrounded by a sea of smiling people who'd come to greet us warmly and welcome us when we arrived in Dembidolo. "You have the support of the people, I see," he said.

We saw why after incredible visits with our sponsored families, seeing firsthand how their lives had transformed because of the program. Blessed by the company of Ethan, Pastor Garamu, and Wakjira, Dembidolo didn't feel so foreign to me this time, but it sure did to Ethan.

"You said there's no way to prepare anyone for Dembidolo, and you were right," Ethan said after our first day there. "The beauty and the tragedy are overwhelming. What you've done here is nothing short of amazing. What you could do, though, is what blows my mind."

Ethan and I stood side by side, watching as the late afternoon sun bathed the village in a golden light. The air was thick with the familiar scents of pungent spices and fresh bread, blending with the hum of life around us. It was the kind of moment that, years ago, would have felt impossible. But now, as we walked through the market square, I saw the fruits of our labor in every smiling face, in every small shop that lined the dusty road.

A man waved to us from his stall, colorful bottles of fragrant oils glistening on the table before him. His smile was wide and proud as he motioned for us to come closer. "This was all because of your program," he said, his eyes full of gratitude and pride. "Before, I had nothing to sell—nothing to provide for my family. But now..." He gestured to the bustling marketplace, filled with women bartering and children running between the stalls. "Now, we have enough. My children are fed, and they go to school."

I glanced over at Ethan. His expression mirrored the swelling emotion in my chest. The man's children stood nearby, clean and bright-eyed, their uniforms neat as they clutched their schoolbooks. It was hard to believe that just a few years ago, this family, like so many others, was on the brink of falling apart.

A few stalls down, we approached a woman who stood behind a small table covered in brightly colored wraps and scarves, each one handwoven with care. "These are beautiful," Ethan said, picking up a wrap and admiring the intricate designs woven into the fabric. The woman beamed, her eyes soft with happiness.

"Thank you," she said, her voice full of emotion. Abebe translated, "Your loan gave me the clay to build my first loom, and now I can sell these at the market. I can keep my children with me. I don't have to choose between feeding them and sending them away. We are a family. We are whole."

A lump formed in my throat. This woman, who was once on the brink of losing everything, could now provide for her family and help other women in the village learn her craft. Mothers and daughters everywhere wore her wraps as symbols of the strength that grew from the roots we had planted.

Farther along, the smell of fresh injera filled the air when we stopped at another humble stand where a man worked quickly, pulling bread from the small clay ovens our loan enabled him to buy. He smiled warmly. "Before this, I had no way to make a living. Now, I sell bread to families here and in the next village. My children are strong, and they love school. My wife's making plans to open her own stall next month. We can dream again."

Dream again. The words echoed in my heart as I looked at the children running through the market, their bellies full, their laughter ringing like music. They were no longer hungry, forced to beg for food or forfeit their education to survive. They were children again, clean, cared for, and thriving in ways that once seemed far out of reach.

Ethan wiped his eyes with his hand. "This is it," he said softly. "This is what hope looks like. What it does."

I nodded, my throat tight with emotion. "This is what God does. It's why we're here."

It wasn't just about loans or small businesses. It wasn't about bread, oil, or scarves. It was about families staying together, surviving, and even thriving after we were gone. Each loan, each small investment, transformed a life, a future, and a family. These people weren't just surviving anymore; they were building something for their children, something sustainable, something hopeful.

I looked around the village, feeling the warmth of the sun on my face and the quiet hum of life all around us. There was peace here. Not the peace of everything being perfect, but the peace of knowing that, for now, things were okay. Families were together. The children were laughing. Hope was alive.

As we walked to the edge of the village, Ethan looked lost in thought. He caught my eye and gave me a small, knowing smile. "This is what you dreamed of, isn't it?"

"It is," I replied, my voice thick with gratitude. "And it's only the beginning."

We stopped, letting the sounds of the village wash over us—the clinking of pots, the quiet conversations, the distant laughter of children. We'd come so far, but there was much more to do. I let myself breathe in the beauty of it all. The beauty of families made whole, and children encouraged to dream of bright futures.

The trip with Ethan ended far too quickly, but something in us had shifted. Ethan experienced the raw, unfiltered truth of life in Ethiopia—the relentless poverty and heartbreak—and, like me, he would never be the same. He witnessed the crushing despair and the glimmer of hope that flickered through our work, igniting something deep within him.

Back home, our bond as friends and partners grew unbreakable. Ethan officially joined the mission, and together, we threw ourselves into our volunteer work with a renewed sense of purpose, convinced that we could make a lasting impact. Over the next few years, we returned to Ethiopia again and again. Each journey took us deeper into the country's heart and expanded our reach. With every trip, our commitment solidified. There was no turning back, not when we could see so many lives transformed right before our eyes.

Under Ethan's steady leadership, the organization flourished. We branched into new regions near Addis Ababa, sponsoring hundreds more families and helping them find sustainable paths forward. What was once a dream became a reality. Families stayed together, children thrived, and hope took root in communities that had once known only struggle.

Yet, despite our success, a shadow loomed over us. Our orphan prevention work was launched under the parent organization that ran the orphanages I visited on my first trip to Ethiopia. The organization did splendid work for many years in international adoptions and orphan care. However, the leadership lost focus over time and struggled to articulate a clear vision to supporters. In addition, there were challenges with effective program management and proper accounting for ministry resources. Tough decisions needed to be made if we were to continue. As the organization's board president, that responsibility fell primarily on me. It was a bitter irony—our near 100% success rate was undeniable. Still, the support we needed to sustain it dwindled.

"Our first mission has always been to those in the greatest need," the director told me more than once, her voice calm as she explained why our funds were shrinking. But it didn't ease the sting. How could I reconcile that, despite our success, we were losing the resources that allowed us to keep families together and give children a future? That money we raised went elsewhere.

Sitting together one evening after another long day of number-crunching, Ethan looked out over the fading light. "It's amazing, isn't it?" he said, his voice full of wonder. "How far we've come."

I nodded, but there was a weight in my chest I couldn't quite shake. "It is," I replied. "But it's not without its challenges. I can't help but feel we're reaching a point where things could change. There's always something around the corner."

Ethan glanced at me, his brow furrowed slightly. "You think trouble's coming?"

I hesitated, then sighed. "I don't know. Maybe. It just feels like whenever things start to really come together, you've got to be ready for the ground to shift beneath you."

The words hung between us, and though we didn't speak of it again, my sense of unease lingered. We had seen countless lives transformed and witnessed miracles where there had been only hopelessness. But now that we reached what felt like a peak—just when everything was finally falling into place—unforeseen challenges emerged. Obstacles that threatened to tear apart everything we had built. Worse, it was all in the hands of other people.

As I looked ahead, shaken by the uncertainty of our circumstances, I couldn't ignore the feeling that something darker was waiting for us just beyond the horizon. It was as though the ground we stood on was shifting, and though we had weathered storms before, this time felt different.

Chapter Nine

Drowning

The need for increased support to sustain our efforts and expand into other vital initiatives pressed down on me like a weight I couldn't shake. Raising funds for a non-profit, even one with as much heart as ours, felt like pushing a boulder uphill. Getting people across the world to engage with a tragedy they couldn't see or touch turned out to be a nearly insurmountable challenge.

The harsh reality settled in. Despite the long hours, the calls, and the emails, many people would never give anything. Not even a little. The burden of this realization grew, casting shadows over my once unshakeable optimism. I tried to stay positive. The mission was worth the struggle, and the people we helped made it worthwhile. But the weight of it all—the fundraising, the uncertainty—began to drown me. It was as though every responsibility was pulling me under—the mission, the families relying on us, my own family at home, and my job. I kept these feelings to myself for a long time, thinking I could somehow outpace the fear if I kept pushing ahead.

"I'm drowning," I finally admitted to Chris one evening after the pressure became too much to bear. "Between the mission, the family, the job—I can't keep my head above water. People are making decisions that are wasting our precious little funds, and there's nothing I can do about it. I don't know how we can go on much longer."

She listened, always a calm anchor in my storms. "We never know what the future holds."

"Maybe I'm not the right person to lead this anymore," I said, the words heavy in my mouth. "It's all gotten so big. I don't know how to get us out of this."

"Maybe you're meant to step down," she said gently. "Or maybe God wants you to hold on a little longer until someone else comes along. But I don't think He's telling you to quit."

Before I could respond, the phone rang. It was Ethan. "I met with the treasurer today. We're in a financial death spiral," he said bluntly, his voice tight with concern. "We've only got a few months of funding left. I don't know how we'll get through this or how it got so bad so fast. Why didn't they tell us sooner?"

I stared at the wall, my mind spinning, the gravity of his words sinking in, trying not to think back to all the times I worried funds were being mishandled but was too busy to do anything about it, focusing on the families we were helping. Most of us were volunteers. Only a few people in Africa and the U.S. were actual employees of the organization, which made things challenging sometimes. The fact was that more and more, Ethan, I, and a few others gave our time and money freely to support the mission we believed in so much, but our volunteer status enabled the powers that be to keep us at arm's length in some ways. Now, ignoring that had put us in this position. My heart clenched as I thought of the people most affected by this sudden turn of events beyond my control.

"What's going to happen to the families relying on us now? We're responsible for them," Ethan asked.

The thought of abandoning them was unbearable. But no matter how hard I tried to find a way out, I couldn't. I felt trapped, like the ground was crumbling beneath me. "I don't know," I admitted.

"We'll run out of funds. We're bleeding that badly. I'm sorry, but unless a miracle happens, we'll have no choice but to shut down. Abebe and Abonesh will have to share the news with the families." His voice broke.

The news was devastating. We had worked hard to get the mission off the ground, but I had failed to find a way to sustain it. Heart heavy, I drafted my resignation and sent it to the board. When no one responded, I felt better, interpreting the silence as approval. Though this hurt my heart, I also felt lighter with the massive weight of responsibility lifted off me. I'd done the right thing, the best thing for the organization.

I tried to find peace with my decision but couldn't get there, even when I distracted myself by doing things with family and friends.

"Mostly, it's hard not knowing what's happening now. I can't stop thinking I could have done more," I told Ethan.

"You did all you could, Jeff. Think of the people we helped, the lives we changed." Although he tried to console me, I could only think about how I failed all those desperate people, crushed by the weight of it. The same cold, suffocating fear that gripped me as a child returned.

Memories rushed back, unbidden, of the day I nearly drowned. The water had been calm and inviting, much like this mission had once felt. But in an instant, an unseen current pulled me under, and I had been left fighting for my life, struggling to stay above the surface.

***

I fought against Lake Minnetonka's icy grip, but the water devoured me like a hungry beast. Reality sunk in—my life might end on this idyllic summer day, once filled with joy and laughter, and I was powerless to stop it.

We'd been out on the lake all day. It couldn't have been a more perfect July day for fishing. My dad, grandpa, uncle, and his best fishing buddies had looked forward to this trip all year, and I was thrilled to tag along. I didn't even mind keeping an eye on my younger brother.

The guys brought all the essentials for a good fishing trip—bait, tackle, beer, and sandwiches—and loaded up a pontoon boat, heading out to hunt the elusive walleye, northern pike, and bass.

The blazing sun climbed high in a cloudless blue sky, and the fish kept biting as we moved slowly around the lake, staying near the edges where the shade and gigantic fish were. One cooler filled with fish and another emptied of beer and soda while the men dove deep into stories, political talk, and jokes reserved for such times. As they carried on, my brother and I entertained ourselves, listening to the men's exaggerated stories, drinking ice-cold sodas, and dangling poles in the water, waiting to hook the big fish we dreamed about.

Pontoons don't have bathrooms. Guys relieve themselves off the side of the boat when the urge calls. But I was small for six years old and shy in front of everyone else, so when I had to go, I held it as long as I could, hoping the fishing would end soon so I could find a toilet. When that didn't happen, and peeing became imminent, whether I wanted it to happen or not, I thought the others were so busy fishing, drinking, and talking that I could sneak out to the front of the pontoon, away from everyone else fishing off the back, and pee without anyone noticing.

At first, my plan worked. No one saw me open the gate and do my business off the boat's platform. I finished as fast as I could, teetering close to the edge. Trying not to make a mess as I helped fill the shimmering lake, I lost my balance. My foot slipped on the slick fiberglass floor.

Not wearing a life jacket, I plunged into the lake like an arrow. Shocked and struggling to understand, I sank quickly.

Time stopped, but muffled laughter and music initially continued.

Fright froze my arms and legs but not my mind, screaming in terror, urging me to swim up to where the air waited to relieve my burning lungs, but I couldn't move.

The deeper I sank, the faster I fell into the lake's depths, my arms floating above me like useless balloons. I desperately wanted to cry out for help, but my nose and mouth filled with silty water when I tried, choking me.

The last thing I saw was my dad, a faraway, shrinking figure in a blurry red T-shirt with his back to me.

Unable to move, even though every nerve vibrated with fear, I disappeared into the lake, alone and helpless. Drowning. Dying.

The world went completely quiet. I screamed silent shrieks of terror while the sun shone cheerily through the water. The shadow from the pontoon stayed comforting and solid above me until the sunlight died abruptly, and darkness swallowed me.

Now, here I was again, drowning. Only this time, it wasn't water pulling me under. It was the weight of responsibility, of uncertainty, of fear that paralyzed me.

About two weeks after I resigned, a colleague of mine, Brad, asked me to meet him for coffee. "I've got something I want to talk to you about," he'd said, his voice casual, though I could sense there was more to it.

A few days later, we met at a small coffee shop, ordered our drinks, and settled in to catch up on work. I was ready to talk shop, eager to distract myself from the mess that had become my life. "Tell me about your new products, Brad," I said, pulling out a notebook, ready to take notes.

But Brad laughed, shaking his head. "Hey man, I'm not here to talk about work. I want to hear about your mission in Ethiopia."

His words caught me off guard. I wasn't ready to dive into that after everything that had happened. "Sure," I replied cautiously, stirring my coffee. "What do you want to know?"

He leaned in, his eyes intent. "Tell me about the families—the kids. Did you see them break free from extreme poverty? Did their lives transform how you dreamed they would when you started?"

His question hit me hard, but as I began to speak, the weight of the mission's failure lifted. I told him about the program's successes, the families we helped, and the incredible transformations I witnessed. The more I spoke, the more animated I became, reliving those moments of joy and hope. "You wouldn't believe the difference in these families. It's nothing short of miraculous."

Brad smiled, his eyes misting over as he wiped away tears. "Hearing you talk about it, I can imagine it. I can feel it. Thank you for sharing. And thank you for all the work you're doing." Then, he reached into his bag, pulled out a checkbook, and wrote a check.

I sat in stunned silence as he slid the check across the table. When I saw the amount, my heart nearly stopped. It was far more than I'd ever expected, far more than I dared ask from anyone.

Brad leaned forward, his finger pointed at me, his voice suddenly firm. "Man, God gave you this vision, but you must be bolder about sharing it with others. You need to tell them like you just told me."

His words hit me with the force of a prophecy, as though God Himself had sent Brad down from a mountaintop to deliver a message I desperately needed to hear. It shook me to my core. I couldn't speak for a moment. I had no heart to tell him I was no longer with the mission and had already quit. I felt like a coward—spineless and faithless, sitting there like a man adrift without purpose.

I left that coffee shop reeling, my mind spinning with questions. Why did this happen after I walked away from what Brad seemed to believe in so deeply? How had I lost sight of the purpose that once fueled me? And most of all, why had I given up when God clearly hadn't?

As I walked slowly to my car, my phone rang. I glanced at the screen. It was one of the mission board members. I hesitated before answering, my resignation still fresh and raw in my mind.

"I've just returned from overseas and received your shocking resignation," she said, her voice laced with concern. "Is there any way for you not to step down and continue serving? We need you."

I felt the familiar weight settle in my chest. "The way things are right now, I don't think so," I replied, the heaviness in my heart reflected in my voice.

I told her about Brad's unexpected donation and how his words reignited something in me, but it wasn't enough to wash away the discouragement that led me to resign. We could not go on as before.

She listened intently, then gently pleaded with me to reconsider and explore a way forward together. "Pray on it," she said softly, her tone full of hope.

"I will," I promised, though doubt clouded my thoughts. We ended the call, and I sighed, leaning against the car door, feeling the weight of the decision still pressing on me.

I opened a voicemail from Ethan. His messages were usually long-winded as he worked through thoughts and ideas, but this was different. His voice was steady and direct. He laid out a plan with clear, concise steps that could help us move forward as a new organization.

There was a boldness in his words that I hadn't heard before, and something about his message cut through the fog of my uncertainty.

I sat in my car and replayed his message. Did I make a mistake stepping down? Had I acted too soon, driven by fear and mounting pressure? Had I given up on something that still had life left in it? Had I given up on God?

For the first time since I resigned, I allowed myself to ask the questions I had avoided. What if this wasn't the end of the mission? What if, instead of stepping away, I had to step back in—this time with renewed clarity, purpose, and direction?

I didn't sleep very well that night, tossing and turning, reminded of Jonah before he was thrown off a boat and sucked up by a whale. Like him, I tossed and turned, swallowed by whale-sized confusion. "Show me the way, God," I prayed.

I opened my daily devotion the following day, still unsettled and unsure of the next step. As I flipped through the pages, the passage for the day caught me off guard: the book of Jonah. I stared at the words in disbelief. *Jonah? Of all scriptures?* It felt like too much of a coincidence to ignore. There had to be a sign in this, something God was trying to tell me—but what?

The weight of Jonah's story pressed on my heart, his running, his fear, his reluctance to accept God's call. My mind swirled with questions. Was I Jonah? Was I running from something I was supposed to face? What was God trying to show me? I shook my head, half in frustration, half in wonder.

Still dazed, I joined a call with Abebe and Abonesh to catch up on how things were going in Africa, dreading the inevitable moment when I would have to tell them I'd resigned. After a few minutes of greetings and progress reports, I told them I was no longer part of the organization.

After a long silence, Abebe said, "I can't believe it. This makes me sad."

Abonesh didn't say anything at all.

I felt horrible. Their shock and sadness were torture. I didn't think it would hit them so hard. They were more than mission partners; they were my dear friends. We'd been through so many things together. So many difficulties, highs, and lows. I was agonized about leaving them and full of doubt. *What have I done?*

Abonesh is one of the most poised, gentle, and graceful women I know. Full of faith and love, she always seems to speak with the voice of an angel from her heart. "God birthed a vision in your heart and made you dream of a river of hope," she said. "He caused it to become a reality. He has given you this calling. You must go forward in faith, and God will provide and show you the way."

I wept as she and Abebe spoke words of encouragement, comfort, and blessings over my life. When we hung up, I never felt so low. I sat for a long time, thinking of Jonah again. It was no coincidence that the scripture was today's reading, but I struggled to find the message.

In the story, God commanded Jonah to preach His word to the city, but Jonah ran. He fled from the task, got caught in a storm, and was trapped inside a whale's belly.

Had I run away, too? I couldn't help but wonder if I had taken the easy way out, sidestepping God's direction when the waters got rough.

As Jonah sank to his lowest, darkest place, swallowed by fear and the depths of the sea, he cried out to God for forgiveness. "But I, with the voice of thanksgiving, will sacrifice to you; what I have vowed I will pay; Salvation belongs to the Lord!" (Jonah 2:9).

It was only when Jonah fully surrendered to God's plan that he was delivered—spit out onto the shore and given a second chance.

Would God give me a second chance too? I asked myself, feeling the question's weight settle in my chest. I was drowning again—though not in water, but in fear, anxiety, and the crushing weight of my responsibilities. The mission, family, and self-doubt felt like it was pulling me under. Was there still a chance for me, like Jonah, to come up for air, to realign with what God wanted me to do despite my fears?

I flashed back to that day on the lake as a kid, flailing in the water, the cold filling my lungs, the surface slipping farther and farther away as I sank deeper. I had been drowning then, too, consumed by fear as death seemed to reach for me. The panic and hopelessness were all too familiar now, even though it wasn't water I fought this time, but my anxious worries.

My dad pulled me from the water before it was too late. I hadn't saved myself; I'd been rescued. Maybe, just maybe, God was ready to do the same for me again. My dad's swift rescue was a poignant symbol of God's unwavering love, which guides life's turbulent seas and shows us the transformative power of resilience, the enduring bonds of faith, and the miracles of hope illuminating our path through life's unpredictable waters.

Looking back, I realized that was the first time God stepped in to save me. As I struggled beneath the surface, it was as if a divine hand reached down, reassuring me that my story was far from over. That moment marked the beginning of a lifelong journey of faith, redemption, and rescue where, time and time again, God's grace rescued me from the depths, no matter how afraid I was or how far from him I wandered.

Mind whirling with new hope and possibilities, I focused on the profound truth, revelations, and possibilities that emerge when life's currents threaten to overwhelm, yet divine intervention and faith hold steadfast. And I put my faith back in God to show me the way forward again.

I'd blown it. Gotten it wrong. Run in the wrong direction. I made an emotional decision to quit based on fear, not faith. And the occasionally crazy events in my life were God's way of getting my attention. I couldn't outrun him. I made a mistake, but God wasn't mad at me. He gently used Brad, Ethan, Abebe, Abonesh, and others to get my attention.

This time, I listened. The message was unmistakable; I needed to un-quit or un-resign. Telling people I changed my mind would be embarrassing, even if I worked out how to do it with the least trouble for anyone.

I told Ethan first. "Over the past few days, God has shown me, through people and His Word, that I am running in the wrong direction. I let pressure and fear get to me and was so afraid of failing that I ran away from God's vision and calling for my life."

"You have been worn out and discouraged," he said. "But God-sized callings can only be fulfilled with God-sized strength and provision. You can't go forward with your strength alone. Turn it over to God and seek to be faithful instead of successful."

"And call out to Him whenever I feel like I'm drowning again," I said with a grin.

"First, you better figure out how to jump back in after resigning," Ethan said, always practical.

Looking over the organization's bylaws again, I found the answer. When a board member resigns, the board must formally accept and document the resignation. Although I'd sent a resignation letter, the board had not replied or taken any action yet, so my resignation wasn't official.

I ran to my computer and wrote a new letter to the board rescinding my resignation. I said we needed to meet to discuss new directions for the organization and set us on a path to avoid running out of funds again.

Relief hit me as soon as I hit send. Unquitting was the right thing to do. I knew it in my bones and heart even as I prayed that I would rise to the challenges ahead. This time, I relinquished control of the outcome to God, accepting that the organization's fate rested in His hands, not mine. My resolve was clear: to remain faithful and fulfill my role, providing hope for families on the brink of despair through the newly focused mission.

Chapter Ten

What Depths of Wisdom in Her Ocean?

The challenges that once drove me to the edge hadn't disappeared; if anything, they multiplied. But this time, fear didn't hold me captive. Instead, a newfound fire surged within me, an unshakable conviction that I was exactly where I was meant to be. Doubt no longer whispered in my ear. I returned not because the road became easier but because I was stronger. I was ready for the battles ahead and wasn't walking alone this time.

The urgency in the room was palpable. We had only weeks of operating funds left, and the weight of our situation pressed hard against me. But as I stood before the board, something shifted. I wasn't here to bow to fear. I was here to fight.

"Would God bring us this far just to see us fail?" I asked, my voice cutting through the silence like a blade. The room was still. I wasn't asking for sympathy. I was daring us all to believe.

"We're looking at the problems instead of the solution," I continued, the fire inside me burning brighter. "If we are not meant to fail, then help will come. But we need to change our focus. We need a Nehemiah moment."

Heads began to nod. "Didn't Nehemiah say, 'The God of Heaven will give us success'?" a board member asked.

I leaned forward. "Yes. He said, 'We are His servants, and we will start rebuilding.' That's what we're going to do."

I couldn't stop thinking about Nehemiah, the prophet who faced the destruction of his beloved Jerusalem. He didn't waver when he saw his city in ruins; he wept, prayed, and rebuilt—against impossible odds. That's what we needed to do. The brokenness I saw in Ethiopia was our Jerusalem. The collapse of families, the endless cycle of poverty—that was our battle. And like Nehemiah, from this brokenness, we were going to rise.

Ethan spoke up, his voice cutting through the tension. "There will always be opposition when you try to build a vision. But look at Nehemiah. He stayed focused on what God called him to do. We've lost that focus. We've been doing the same things, hoping for a miracle."

He was right. I felt the truth of his words deep in my gut. "It's time to do things differently," I said, my determination solidifying. "From now on, everything we do must empower families long-term. We've seen the success of micro-loans and small businesses. That's our path forward, our new mission."

Suddenly, the room buzzed with energy. Our hopelessness dissolved as we laid out a clear plan. We broke it down into four steps: Embrace, Equip, Empower, Employ. Every step a victory.

"When we embrace families teetering on the edge of collapse with compassion and sponsorship, that's our first win," I declared.

Ethan scribbled notes, his excitement growing. "And then we equip them with what they need to stabilize—food, clothes, essentials. Win two."

"From there, we empower them with a micro-loan, giving them the tools to build a future," I added. "That's win three."

"And the final win," Ethan said, eyes bright, "is when they can employ themselves, running their own successful businesses and breaking the chains of poverty for good."

The excitement in the room was electric. We saw the way forward. This wasn't just survival; this was revival. We found our focus, and now we needed others to see it with their own eyes.

"Like Nehemiah, people need to witness the brokenness to understand it truly," Ethan said. "They have to see it."

"Exactly," I agreed. "We'll bring people to Ethiopia. Not for a mission trip but a vision trip. They're coming to see the work, to experience it firsthand. That's how they'll catch the vision—by seeing it with their own eyes."

The burden of failure that hung so heavily on us for so long lifted. We weren't alone in this mission anymore. We knew God would bring others to walk this path with us, people ready to see the need and help carry the vision.

Weeks later, boarding the plane for our first vision trip, the financial pressure still loomed. But my faith was rock solid. This mission belonged to God, not us, and He would provide the way.

And He did. After the trip, one of the vision members pulled us aside. He and his wife wanted to become vision partners, and their commitment, in the form of a check, was the exact amount we needed to close our financial gap to the penny.

"I guess God isn't going to let this mission fail," Ethan said, his voice thick with emotion.

I smiled, feeling the weight lift off my shoulders completely. "Because it's His vision. And we're just here to carry it forward."

For the first time in a long time, I felt hopeful and unshakably confident. We were on the right path. God called us here, and with Him leading, there was no limit to what we could accomplish.

We named our new mission Family Hope International.

***

Managing the mission's growth and expansion filled my days, and our bustling household of children filled my heart. Our family, with its laughter and chaos, felt whole. The notion of further expanding it didn't cross my mind anymore. My contentment and sense of completeness felt immovable.

When people asked about our openness to adopting more children, I offered the same practiced answer: we are always open to God's plans. But inwardly, I was sure. We were full. Our family was whole. I believed if God intended to place another child in our lives, He would make that call unmistakable, something I couldn't ignore or misinterpret.

And then came that sunlit Saturday afternoon, ordinary in its warmth and quiet, when everything changed.

Chris came into my home office, her face illuminated with excitement and something deeper, something reverent. She held her laptop as though it carried a fragile secret.

"Jeff! You have to see this," she said, hushed but urgent. She set the laptop down in front of me and paused on a still frame of a dark-haired boy, maybe eight or nine, his face soft and expectant. She hit play.

"This is Caleb," a woman's voice narrated. "He's one of many orphans here."

The boy, Caleb, held up a drawing. It was simple, childlike, yet achingly familiar: a house with a family in front of it, arms open.

He spoke softly in Chinese, and the woman translated, "He says he had a dream about the family in this picture. There are nine other children, all different from him. They live in a big house."

The breath caught in my throat. I leaned closer, a sudden, strange tightening in my chest. The house he had drawn looked remarkably like ours—an American house, sprawling, with enough room for a family our size.

"That looks like our house," I said, half to myself. "And we have nine kids."

Chris's eyes sparkled. "Just wait."

The woman in the video asked Caleb to explain the drawing further. He pointed to one of the children and said a name that sounded like Joshua.

I looked up at Chris, disbelief flooding my face. "We have a Joshua."

Caleb pointed to another child and said what sounded like Angelina.

"We have an Angelie," Chris whispered, her voice trembling.

A chill ran down my spine. How could this child, on the other side of the world, know our family, our names? We hadn't connected with this agency. The video was made by an orphanage in China and posted without any link to us. And yet, this boy dreamed of our family, of a life he could not possibly have known.

"How can this be?" I asked, my voice shaking. "How did he dream of a family like ours? Nine children—how would he even understand that? China has a one-child policy. Families like ours don't exist there."

"It must mean something, Jeff. It has to."

I sat in silence, the weight of it all crashing over me. I thought of the dreams that guided me in the past, those inexplicable nudges that could only come from God. This was no different. This was a message as clear as any I'd ever received. This little boy in China—he'd dreamed of a family, and it was ours.

My heart softened, yielding to a truth I couldn't deny. "Sometimes," I said softly, "the hardest thing to say to God is yes. But this is a yes. Why don't you see what more you can learn about him?"

As we sat, the decision began to settle into place. God's plan unfolded again before us, and I knew, deep in my soul, that this was His call. Caleb, this boy with his dream, was meant to be part of our family.

Chris, her eyes filled with emotion, nodded. "There's another boy," she said. She played a second video, this time of a smaller child, bright-eyed and laughing, from another orphanage. We watched the video in silence, then returned to Caleb's.

We prayed, talked, and began the adoption process for both boys the next day. Though they were not biological brothers, we knew they were meant to grow up together, bound by their shared heritage and the journey that would soon bring them into our family.

Months passed, and the process unfolded as adoption processes do—slowly, painstakingly, but with purpose. When the approval came, Chris asked her close friend Colleen to join her for the trip to China to bring the boys home. When they arrived, the culture shock hit them like it had hit me all those years ago. The orphanages, the starkness, the overwhelming sense of loss and hope intertwined—it was all there.

"These kids," Chris said to me when she returned, her eyes heavy with the weight of it, "they're giving up so much. They're leaving behind everything they know. Their language, their culture, all of it. It's such a loss, even though they're gaining a family."

I held her close, feeling the depth of her heart. "They'll have us," I said quietly. "And we'll do everything we can to help them adjust, to keep who they are intact while they discover who they'll become."

As the months passed, Caleb and Isaac—though not brothers by birth—grew close as if they were bound by something deeper than blood. Caleb adjusted quickly, full of light and curiosity, easily stepping into the life he once dreamed of. Isaac, quieter and more reserved, struggled at first, the enormity of the change weighing heavily on him. But in time, he, too, began to thrive.

Our openness to God's call once again expanded our family. Eleven children now, yet it felt right as if Caleb's dream had always been our destiny. What started as a moment of disbelief had grown into something undeniable: God's vision for our family was bigger than anything I could have imagined.

With the boys finally settling, it was time to return to Ethiopia. As I boarded the plane, I reflected on my life's beautiful, winding path. The connection to the world's most vulnerable, its children, started as a calling, but it became the heartbeat of my life, woven into the very fabric of who I had become.

***

In the years that followed, as we worked in Korah and Dembidolo, our organization discovered profound truths about transforming lives. Every family we helped move from the brink of hopelessness to self-sustainability taught us something new. Our focus on small business ventures was no longer just an experiment or a strategy in a larger mission. It became the lifeblood of our entire mission, empowering families to rewrite their futures.

As we expanded into new areas around Addis, the ripple effect of this approach became undeniable. Hope was no longer a fleeting promise but a tangible reality.

On one trip, we visited several sponsored families, walking through the village to a group of huts where many people lived together so our vision team members could see our families' living conditions and learn about their lives.

In one tiny hut, we visited an extremely old woman who greeted us from a makeshift bed tucked into the corner of the room.

"She is over 100 years old," Abebe told us, holding her hand and speaking softly. "Bedridden for the last twelve years. Here on her own."

The woman wore a peaceful expression, though malnutrition and disease had ravaged her. Her eyes shone brightly as she looked at me, and I wondered how so much joy remained in a body so terribly wasted and deformed by poverty and illness.

"Isn't there somewhere she could go to be cared for?" Megan asked, struggling to find solutions in this place where almost none existed.

The pastor with us that day shook his head. "No care facilities exist to care for people in such a position, so we do our best to bring relief, hoping something will change and more help will come for souls like hers. We pray." He smiled gently. "And sometimes, people like you come to us."

The stench of waste and decay overwhelmed my senses. I could not imagine living, day in and day out, in this room, in this horrible, hopeless place, lying on a urine-soaked mattress, dependent on what others would do for me.

"Is there anything you would like to have? Something you need we can get for you?" Dave, another team member, asked.

The old woman considered the question for a long moment. "I have everything I need. I can't think of a thing," she said through Abebe.

"Everything you need? You have nothing. Surely you could use a blanket or a new mattress?" Dave said.

A new hut, a fridge, a car, 401K, and a vacation home would help. I thought about the endless list of what most Americans would ask for if offered anything.

Faced with this woman dying in a bed with nothing yet asking for nothing, I wondered what I could learn from her, accepting things instead of constantly struggling to find solutions to change them.

What does she know that I don't?

"What does she have?" Dave asked incredulously, sweeping his arm around the sad, empty space. Like many people faced with such hopelessness, he'd grown angry, his voice louder as he searched for a way to help.

Abebe smiled at the woman's quick reply. "She says she has Jesus," he said. "He is everything and gives her all she needs."

I also have Jesus, but I have everything else life has to offer—and more. It's undeniable that these things contribute to my happiness and well-being.

If Jesus were all I had, would He be enough?

As a former pastor and mission leader, I was expected to know God intimately and guide others toward Him. Yet, my relationship with Him sometimes felt transactional, as if He were a spiritual genie granting my desires. Would I still worship and adore Him if He gave me nothing in return? If my life was filled with despair, pain, poverty, and illness?

My heart quietly answered, "No," and with that came shame and a profound realization. *She knows Jesus in a way I don't.*

"This woman's greatest joy and longing is Jesus. He is all she has, always in this room, always with her. Don't you feel Him?" the pastor asked, beaming with faith.

What if the noise and excess drowned out God's presence in my daily life? The thought lingered as we left the old woman's home.

Many of the poor I met that day possessed more joy than most Americans and far more faith in God. *What do they know in their poverty that we, with all our advantages, don't know?*

"Maybe we have a different type of poorness." Dave, who seemed more relaxed now, pondered after we left the old woman's home. "Have we lost the ability to feel the pain and hurts of the neediest? Has our consumer culture or technology caused us to lose our intimate relationship with God and the ability to touch and feel what truly matters in our faith?"

"In some ways, many wealthier people are more diseased and poorer than even our leper brothers and sisters for their lack of true faith and understanding of the gift of Jesus in our lives. The power of genuine, unfiltered belief," the pastor suggested.

I kept thinking I had so much more than the poor in Africa, often haunted by my wealth and success in the face of the problems others suffered, but did I?

"Scripture says God has chosen the poor of this world to be rich in faith. They are richer than us if what they possess brings them such joy and comfort of soul in their physical, yet temporary misery," Abebe said. "And you are richer for having served them."

"The poverty and deprivation are so shocking," Meghan said several times. Like most of us, she saw no solution to the problems.

"It's worse than on TV," Dave agreed.

Many of us wiped tears away as we walked around, greeted, and sometimes hugged the people we met, who were always kind and welcoming, continually expressing gratitude for our visit. Smiling. Laughing. Grateful. So happy to meet us. So thankful to God for bringing us to them. For the miracle of another day.

In a tiny hut, we found two women talking. One was in deep despair, sobbing. Without understanding anything, I felt the hopelessness and hurt.

Abonesh, who still led many trips like this, said the ladies were close friends and neighbors. We sponsored the woman who was not crying. "She had no idea we were going to visit today. This mother, her friend, has no job, money, or food. She's run out of everything," she explained. "The crying woman came to tell her friend she is taking her two little children to her home village tomorrow to abandon them on the streets, hoping someone might pity them and give them food in a larger town."

Looking around the room, I saw the rest of our team felt as stunned as me, watching a family about to disintegrate. Two little ones were about to fall into the river and become practical orphans, orphans with one or both parents still living, something widespread in all impoverished countries. When parents can't feed and care for their children, the choice becomes death or abandonment.

Abonesh gently spoke to the weeping mother, learning more about her misery. The mother and her children were in desperate circumstances, in terrible condition.

Our team stood by, shocked and saddened, until Judy, from Boise, deeply affected by the woman's desperate situation, moved to her and embraced her. "This is my family," she said as tears of joy flowed from many watching eyes.

Abonesh explained what was happening to the crying woman and told her she would not have to abandon her kids on the streets. She explained about our program and how the woman hugging her would help keep her family together.

We witnessed the most miraculous and radical transformation on the woman's face when she realized Judy embraced her with hope. She wouldn't have to leave or abandon her children. They could have a future. They would not drown.

Judy later said, "My heart broke. I asked if I could help this woman keep her children, and Our Father answered, just in time. He sent me to Ethiopia. Jeff, remember before we left for the trip when I told you that God would show me who my family was and that I would sponsor them?" Judy beamed.

"I do! I told you I was sure He would, and he did." I grinned.

"When I gave her the gifts I brought for the family I'd sponsor, I couldn't speak. The emotion was overwhelming," Judy said later. "I wanted to tell her that God had heard her and how much He loved her, but, in the end, all I could do was cry and hold her."

"She saw firsthand how God opened your eyes to her need, your ears to her cries, and your heart to her pain," I said.

"I am truly stunned by what happened," Judy said. "That woman could have gone to anyone, but she went to someone in your program. The FHI program's help is like drops of water in the ocean. Helping even one person in the smallest way will cause a ripple effect."

"You stepped out in bold faith and met a need God prepared for you, and you moved a mountain of poverty for another soul and saved a family from destruction," I said. "A family preserved is an orphan prevented. You changed the world for them when support was a matter of life and death."

When we left, Judy asked, "Does this sort of thing happen often, where mothers feel forced to abandon their children?"

"There are many stories of small children abandoned on the street or newborn babies left in the bushes on the side of the road. If nobody finds them in time, the hyenas will eventually come and find them," Abonesh said. "They would rather give their child a swift death than see them die a slow and painful one through starvation."

"I can't even wrap my head around doing such a thing." Judy's voice held the sadness and confusion I'd heard before. "Why don't they leave? Why are they there to start with? I can't comprehend how these things happen and how people try to live without food, water, or hope."

"The only help they get is from family and friends. So, if they go somewhere else, they'd have no one. The very act of leaving affects their survival odds. It would be catastrophic for them to leave the prison they are in because their families are there with them. Extreme poverty truly imprisons them with no hope of escape," I explained.

"They just want to keep their families together." Judy's heart understood before her mind did. "Their lives, experiences, are so far away from mine. Feeling like you have no choice but to leave a baby for wild animals to eat. Honestly, even now, I cannot fathom the pain leading to such a place. Why don't they have help? Why can't they leave the baby at a hospital or orphanage?"

"They have no resources to travel. No knowledge of anything but the solutions of others before them. No help. Shame plays a part sometimes. So many babies come from rape or a sudden change of situation like when a husband dies," Abonesh said.

"I know many people who think they have problems or aren't doing well financially. But compared to the rest of the world, most of us are rich beyond belief," Judy said. "I can't believe more people don't help, that you, Ethan, and a few others volunteer so much time and money while so many do nothing."

"Some of the happiest people I've met are the poorest. It makes you think, doesn't it?" I shook my head. "Most people just don't understand the problem enough or realize how little effort or money it takes to make huge changes in the lives of the people here."

"There are so many contrasts in this place. Such beauty yet so much brokenness," Judy said.

"You never run out of stories about personal struggles here," I said, reflecting on the countless lives shaped by adversity. "One story that lingers in my mind is that of a young mother named Entenesh. Even by Ethiopian standards, she was tiny, her frame delicate beneath the weight of her responsibilities. Accompanying her was her daughter, a spirited girl of about four years."

Their home was a tiny hut assembled from scraps of corrugated metal that were haphazardly wired together, creating walls that barely shielded them from the outside world. Inside, the space felt stifling, with little room to breathe, let alone thrive. Entenesh struggled to earn enough money to cover the rent, making it impossible to provide adequate food for herself and her precious child. They were on the brink of despair, clinging to life in a remote area where hope was scarce.

"The hyenas come many nights," she shared with a mixture of fear and resilience in her voice. Her eyes widened as she recounted the terror of those nights. "Several times, they tried to break into my hut while I held the door shut with every ounce of strength I could muster, praying that I could keep them out." It was hard to fathom how this slight woman could summon such determination, but she insisted that failure was not an option. If the hyenas had managed to break through, they would have savaged her and her child, leaving death in their wake. That flimsy piece of scrap metal was their only barrier against a horrifying fate.

"She explained that hyenas are not just ordinary beasts; they are monstrous predators, more menacing than any dog or wolf. Known to attack and consume people, their presence looms like a shadow in the lives of those who live in these vulnerable conditions. For Entenesh and many like her, the threat of a hyena attack was not a distant horror;

it was a common experience, a chilling reality that heightened the struggle for survival," I said.

"What happened to her?" Judy asked.

"Thankfully, we found her family a sponsor and moved her and her child to another, more secure home," I said.

"Recently, Entenesh graduated from our program with a successful small business. No more sleepless nights fighting off hyenas or hunger for her!" Abonesh smiled.

"Everyone here looks poor and needs help," Judy said. "How do you decide who to bring into the program?"

"Americans would have a hard time assessing who is the neediest," Ethan replied. "So, we rely on the help of the local community leaders and pastors to help our staff identify the most desperate families in their areas. We can't help all of them, so we focus on helping the neediest. For us to bring a family into our program, we must assess that they will not make it, that they are going to drown and disintegrate, and the children will soon become orphaned."

We gathered for dinner after a brutal day for our team, filled with overwhelming sights and emotions. Sharing our stories, the air was thick with the weight of what we witnessed. Tears flowed freely, and raw emotions surfaced.

"The need is so vast," Judy said quietly, her voice trembling with sorrow. "It's like an endless ocean of poverty, with so many drowning, and we're just a small lifeboat. How can we do enough before it's too late? I want to think we can, but I'm having difficulty believing."

Her question lingered long after dinner, echoing in the minds of us all. The following day, as we packed up and set off for the uncharted southern region of Ethiopia—a place I had yet to explore—there was a palpable sense of both trepidation and determination. We were venturing into the unknown, not just across unfamiliar landscapes but also within ourselves, facing challenges that would test our limits in ways we had yet imagined. The journey ahead would push us beyond what we knew into territories both geographic and deeply personal.

Months before, when planning the trip itinerary, Abebe asked, "Why don't we consider expanding Family Hope into remote areas in the southern regions of Ethiopia? I have strong contacts there and many friends pleading with us to come and help."

Let's do it!" I said, adding it to our itinerary. We decided to visit Gutumuma, a remote agricultural area, first.

Our little group drove for miles, eventually turning off the main road onto a small, dusty one with endless potholes. It was clogged with donkey carts overloaded with entire families, and our progress was slow.

Most of the people in the southern region of Ethiopia are from the Oromo Tribe, quite different from the Amhara Tribe in Addis and our other project areas, though they make up most of the ethnic population of Ethiopia. Their rich culture is reflected in their traditional clothing, often made from natural materials such as cotton, leather, and animal skins. Men wear toga-like robes, while women wear long, wrap skirts, shawls, or scarves decorated with intricate beadwork and embroidery.

Wide-eyed and energized by the feast of new sights and sounds, we eventually arrived at a little church inside a walled and gated compound in Gutumuma.

Gutumuma was a village at the world's edge, or so it seemed. Nestled deep in the southern reaches of Ethiopia, it felt almost hidden from time itself. The land stretched wide and open in this place, untouched by modern life. The earth here was a rich, deep red, cracked, and dry from months without rain, yet it exuded a sense of quiet resilience. Sparse acacia trees dotted the landscape, their twisted branches casting thin shadows across the parched ground, while the hills in the distance rolled gently, fading into the horizon.

The air in Gutumuma was thick with the smell of earth and smoke. Fires crackled from small clay ovens where women prepared simple meals, and the faint scent of eucalyptus drifted down from nearby groves. The village was modest, made up of round, thatched-roof huts clustered together in organic order, each symbol of survival against the odds. Chickens pecked at the dirt between the homes, and goats roamed freely, their bleats mixing with the distant chatter of children playing near the river.

Life in Gutumuma was simple but challenging. The village had long struggled with scarcity—of food, clean water, and opportunities. The people wore their hardships on their faces, etched deep into the lines of their skin by years of drought and labor. But they also had a quiet dignity, an unwavering will to endure. This was a place where survival was not a given but a daily challenge. Yet, somehow, there was still joy in the small things—a child's laugh, the sharing of a meal, the warmth of the community gathered around a fire at night.

When we first came to Gutumuma, it felt like stepping into a forgotten world where the struggles were raw and unrelenting. But as we spent more time there, I began to see the spark of hope that flickered beneath the surface. Our programs could bring more than just aid; they brought the promise of something better—a future that could be built, brick by brick, right here in the dry soil.

Revitalized by our agricultural training, small farms would sprout with new crops, pushing up green shoots where there had only been dust once. Clean water sources, dug with the help of local labor, would change the rhythm of daily life, allowing women and children to spend less time walking miles to the river and more time learning, working, and dreaming. It wasn't much, but it was a start.

Gutumuma had a long way to go, and the journey ahead was still uncertain. But the people here, toughened by the land and united in their struggle, believed their future didn't have to mirror their past. There was something profound in the quiet, stubborn hope of a village starting to fight for something more.

The people of Gutumuma greeted our team with overwhelming warmth, their enthusiasm filling the air. They sang and shouted in high-pitched, joyful tones, letting out the traditional cry of "Lelelelelelele!" that echoed through the village.

Most women were Muslim, and many had eight to twelve children. Their lives were marked by hardship but also by unshakable resilience. Despite their poverty, they carried themselves with strength radiating from their bodies and spirits. When they hugged you, they hugged you, their thin arms wrapping around you with a surprising and fierce embrace that left no doubt of the depth of their welcome.

Some of their customs caught me off guard, like how they would spit lightly on your face as a gesture of blessing, doing it several times during each visit. It was unexpected but genuine, a tradition rooted in their culture. Though they initially surprised me, I understood their blessings' deep significance.

Our time with these remarkable women was unforgettable. They had so little, but their spirits were rich with joy, their laughter infectious, their kindness boundless. I would carry the memory of their strength and joy with me into other remote places, and I looked forward to the day I might return to see them again.

Our work was expanding, like the roots of a stubborn tree that digs deeper into the ground, refusing to give up. We were helping people build their lives, business by business. No matter how audacious it once seemed, the vision would become a reality in this dry and distant corner of the world.

As I boarded the plane back to the States, the images of the children in Africa stayed with me—bright, smiling faces full of hope and families reunited, thriving. It had been a rewarding trip, watching the fruits of years of work take root, but now my heart ached for home. Leaving was always bittersweet; Africa had become a part of me, and the children we served felt like an extension of my family. But as the miles stretched between us and the familiar hum of the engines filled my ears, my thoughts turned toward Chris and the kids. I missed the noise, the chaos, and the way our home always seemed full to bursting with life and love.

Whenever I felt that ache for home, I thought of our camping trips to Nehalem Bay. The mere thought of those summer days, packed into a truck and trailer with eleven kids and half our belongings, filled me with warmth. There was something magical about those trips, something that brought our already close family even closer. The long drives, the smell of the ocean mingling with campfire smoke, and the kids' laughter as they raced along the dunes on bikes were pure joy. I could almost feel the cool breeze coming off the Pacific and hear the fire crackling as we huddled around, roasting marshmallows, teasing each other about who had the best s'mores technique.

I smiled, eager to return to the thick of it. Life with eleven kids was exhausting, but that kind of exhaustion left you content at the end of the day. And those camping trips? They were the perfect reminder that, no matter how wild things got, there was no place I'd rather be than surrounded by my family, living in the beautiful chaos we'd created.

Chapter Eleven

Chaotic Harbor, Sheltered from the Storms

"Is this everything?" Chris asked, glancing over at the pile of bikes, chairs, and coolers outside the garage. Her hands rested on her hips, her tired but amused eyes surveying the chaos before her. Eleven kids darted around the driveway, their voices mixing in a blur of excited chatter.

I shoved the last tent into the van. "Probably not," I said with a grin. "But we'll figure out what we forgot halfway down I-5, as usual."

Chris laughed, shaking her head. "Every time."

Every year, it was the same. We'd swear to be more organized for the next trip, and every year, we'd still be frantically packing ten minutes before departure. I glanced at our massive, red Chevy van—affectionately dubbed Big Red—hitched to our even larger trailer. It was a beast. Maneuvering it along the Oregon Coast with a dozen bikes hanging off the back was a miracle.

"Mom! I call back seat!" came a cry from near the trailer.

"No, I called it first!" another voice retorted, and before long, five kids were fighting over the prime van real estate.

I caught Chris's eye. "You sure we're ready for this?" I asked with mock uncertainty.

She raised an eyebrow. "Too late to back out now."

Twenty minutes later—after two arguments, a spilled juice box, and an impromptu search for a missing sandal—we were finally on the road. As the kids settled in for the long drive, we hit play on the DVD player. Predictably, the kids picked *The Long, Long Trailer*, the 1950s comedy we watched on every road trip since our first adoption. I didn't mind. The film had become a family tradition, and its humor was somehow even funnier with every viewing.

"I swear, if you start acting like Lucy when we park this trailer, I'm leaving you in the woods," I teased Chris, glancing sideways as we cruised down the freeway.

She shot me a mock glare. "Hey, Lucy was doing her best!"

"Sure, sure. Just keep those hand signals clear." I winked, knowing full well that backing the trailer into a campsite was one of our most stressful—and hilarious—adventures every trip.

Hours later, we finally arrived at Nehalem Bay after a long journey peppered with snack requests, bathroom stops, and the inevitable "Are we there yet?" chorus.

Nehalem Bay is a place that feels like it exists outside of time, a little slice of heaven tucked between the rugged Oregon Coast and the endless stretch of blue-gray Pacific. As soon as we pulled into the campground, the smell of saltwater and pine wrapped around us, like the land welcoming us back. The bay sits cradled by towering dunes, their sandy peaks dotted with seagrass that dance in the breeze. Beyond them, the ocean roars endlessly, its waves crashing with a rhythm that soothes even the most restless of hearts.

The campground itself was a mix of nature's untamed beauty and the comforting sense of routine that came with setting up camp. Tall, weathered pines stretched toward the sky, offering patches of shade that felt like a reprieve from the sun on those rare warm Oregon afternoons. Narrow paths wove toward the beach between the trees, where the kids raced ahead, their laughter carried on the wind. It was the kind of place where the days melted together between your toes, the sound of gulls overhead, and the soft glow of campfires flickering through the evening mist. It was wild, raw, and simple, yet it always felt like home.

The cool sea breeze washed over us as we pulled into the campsite, and the kids were instantly excited. I braced myself for the next hurdle: parking this monster.

"All right, everyone out," I called as the kids tumbled out of the van like a tidal wave of energy, racing each other toward the beach that stretched just beyond the dunes.

Chris stood ready to guide me, her hands poised for directions. "Just take it slow," she called, her voice calm, though we both knew this could turn into a full-scale disaster any second.

The trailer lurched backward, and I winced as it started to veer off the path. "No, no, no, the other way!" Chris motioned wildly, her arms waving in a way that reminded me exactly of Lucy.

"Like I said, Lucy!" I yelled out the window, laughing.

She threw her hands up dramatically.

It took a few tries—and a lot of laughing—but eventually, we got the trailer positioned. My boys, always eager to help, scrambled to assist with the setup. Each had their own little task—holding a cord here, adjusting a tarp there. The girls were already diving into the trailer, helping their mom with the unpacking, while the youngest made a beeline for the dunes, their laughter echoing through the campsite.

As the sun dipped low, casting a golden glow over the ocean, the familiar scent of campfire smoke filled the air. I sat back in my camp chair, sipping the cup of coffee Chris handed to me, watching our kids roam free. Bikes zipped by, feet kicked up sand, and distant giggles carried on the wind. It was loud, chaotic, and the farthest thing from peaceful. But it was our kind of chaos.

Chris plopped down in the chair next to me, a tired but satisfied smile on her face. "Well, we did it," she said, taking a long breath.

"Barely," I added, stretching my legs before me. "But yeah. We did."

We both sat in comfortable silence for a moment, the waves crashing in the distance, kids shouting as they built sandcastles and raced their bikes along the beach paths. I glanced over at Chris, shaking my head in wonder. "You know, we're living some kind of crazy life."

She laughed softly. "And I wouldn't trade it for the world."

Me neither. Something about these moments—campfires under the stars, sticky fingers from s'mores, and kids tucked into sleeping bags after a long day of sun and sea—felt like pure magic. Sure, it was exhausting, and sometimes things went spectacularly wrong, but the laughter and love that filled our campsite every summer made it all worth it.

The kids were still running wild as the sun began to dip behind the dunes, casting long shadows across the campsite. Their laughter carried on the breeze. I sat back in my chair, stretching my legs out and feeling the warmth of the campfire, which started to ease the tension in my shoulders. Moments like these were rare and treasured. I relaxed and let my mind and body rest.

Chris joined me, her eyes scanning the chaos around us. "So much for that peaceful camping trip you promised," she teased, nudging my arm.

I chuckled, taking a sip of coffee. "I think that dream died somewhere between the spilled juice boxes and the missing tent poles."

She leaned back, a soft smile spreading across her face. "You know, there are easier ways to spend a vacation. We could've gone somewhere with fewer bikes and sand."

"Maybe. But where's the fun in that?" I said, my eyes following Caleb, racing his sister around the campground on bikes. "Besides, you know this madness is what we're made for."

Chris glanced at me, her smile deepening. "Yeah, I guess we are."

There was a truth in that, one I never really said aloud but always knew deep down. Sure, having eleven kids meant chaos—constant, unrelenting chaos—but it also meant love, laughter, and moments like this, where the world felt full in the best possible way.

The fire crackled between us, and Chris tucked her feet beneath her, relaxing into the quiet moment. "You know," she began thoughtfully, "sometimes I think about how all this came together. How we went from having one kid to, well, a bushel."

I smiled. "Yeah, it's been a wild ride, hasn't it?"

"It's funny how, in the middle of all the craziness, you realize this is exactly where you're supposed to be." Her voice was soft but certain.

I nodded, feeling the same truth deep in my chest. "Yeah, it's like...I don't know, like all of this," I gestured to the campsite, the kids, the trailer, "spills over from something bigger. It's like how I am with the kids back in the orphanages in Africa—it flows from here, from family. From God."

Chris smiled, a warmth spreading across her face. "Exactly."

Ever since our first adoption, something shifted inside me. I wasn't just parenting a family; I was living out my faith in every little moment, every scraped knee, every bedtime prayer, and every bike ride down the Oregon Coast. Raising these kids and reaching out to others along the way became an extension of that faith—a natural, joyful outpouring of the love God filled me with.

I thought of my work in Africa—those long days spent with orphaned children who needed more than food and shelter. They needed a family, a place to belong, a love that didn't come with conditions. It wasn't all that different from the kind of love we gave our kids daily. It was the kind of love that meant running around chasing bikes, burning your fingers on marshmallow sticks, and even forgetting some of the tent poles.

Chris seemed to be reading my thoughts. "It's all connected, isn't it?" she said, watching the fire flicker. "The way you love them. The way you love us."

"Yeah," I murmured. "God didn't just give us these kids to love, but a whole world full of them. And somehow, He gave us the heart to handle it all—even when it feels impossible."

The next moment, as if to prove my point, we heard a shout from behind us.

"Dad! Caleb's stuck in the tree!" Andrew called, clearly more amused than alarmed.

I turned around, and sure enough, there was Caleb, legs dangling from a low-hanging branch of a pine tree, grinning down at us like he'd just conquered Everest.

Chris shook her head, laughing. "Should we save him or let him figure it out?"

"I'm pretty sure we're legally obligated to save him," I said with a grin, getting up from my chair. "I'll handle this one."

As I made my way over to the tree, Caleb gave me a sheepish grin. "Sorry, Dad."

I reached up, easily pulling him down. "What'd I say about climbing trees, Bud?"

"Not to do it?" he said, scratching his head. "But I wasn't going that high."

"Uh-huh," I said, ruffling his hair. "Next time, maybe try not to get stuck, okay?"

He nodded, racing to rejoin the other kids, his little adventure already forgotten.

When I returned to the campfire, Chris had already passed out marshmallows. The kids crowded around the firepit, eager to roast their treats. I sat back down, watching them skewer with too much enthusiasm, sending the occasional flaming marshmallow into the air.

"Watch out! That one's on fire!" I called, but my warning was drowned out by the loud chorus of laughter as the offending marshmallow went up in flames. "Try for a nice golden brown."

Chris leaned over, her voice low. "You realize half of them are just going to eat the charred bits straight off the stick, right?"

I sighed, feigning exasperation. "And we'll pick burnt sugar from their hair for days. But hey, it's tradition."

She laughed, and I couldn't help but laugh with her. Because even though it was messy and chaotic, these were the moments that mattered. Our kids would carry these memories long after the s'mores were eaten and the tents packed up.

As exhausted and sun-kissed kids crowded around the fire, roasting marshmallows and telling stories, their faces glowing in the firelight, I looked around at each of them—eleven beautiful, unique personalities—and felt my heart swell with gratitude.

The campfire burned low. One by one, the kids started to drift off, collapsing into sleeping bags, exhausted and happy. I sat there for a long time, holding Chris's hand, the day's weight slowly lifting off my shoulders.

"You know," she said softly, leaning into me, "there's something pretty special about all this. Not just the camping but all of it. The life we've built together."

I squeezed her hand. "Yeah. It's something, all right."

We sat there in the quiet, the only sound the distant roar of the ocean and the soft crackling of the fire. I thought about the journey we'd been on—from raising Brittany on our own to adopting kids from all walks of life, from my time spent working in Africa to the everyday chaos of raising this big, beautiful family.

It wasn't always easy. There were days when exhaustion felt like it might swallow me whole. But in the stillness of that night, surrounded by the people I loved most in the world, I knew without a doubt that this was precisely where I was meant to be.

As I watched the fire embers glow faintly, I leaned over to Chris, whispering, "You know, we could probably handle a few more if you think about it."

She raised an eyebrow, her mouth twitching into a grin. "A few more what, exactly?"

"Kids. Bikes. S'mores. All of it."

She laughed, resting her head on my shoulder. "You're crazy."

"Yeah, well, I blame God for that," I said, smiling into the dark. "He's the one who keeps making my heart bigger."

***

When I stepped off the plane in Africa the next time, my memories of Nehalem Bay were still fresh. Even though the camping trip had ended, its simplicity lingered, a quiet echo in the chaos that awaited me. The memories of the kids' laughter as they raced through the dunes and the rhythm of the waves crashing on the shore grounded me as I turned my attention back to Ethiopia.

Our time by the Oregon coast reminded me of what we fought for—family, connection, and a sense of belonging. Halfway across the world, a different kind of mission awaited in Ethiopia. The contrast couldn't have been starker—where the peace of the coast left me renewed, Ethiopia's vast, diverse landscape brought its own challenges. Our mission had grown, stretching into regions as far as Dembidolo in the west and Shashemene in the south. With every new step forward, we faced the complexity of preserving families amidst cultural tensions, political conflict, and the constant struggle for stability. As the memories of our family camping trip faded, I felt a renewed sense of purpose stirring within me. The work in Ethiopia was never easy, but like our time at Nehalem Bay, it was worth every effort.

Chapter Twelve

Mysterious Undertows

With each new initiative, we redoubled our efforts to preserve families and prevent the tragedy of orphanhood in every corner of Africa we touched. As we ventured into uncharted territory, the seeds of hope we sowed took root, blossoming into tangible impact far beyond our reach. The promise of change and transformation fueled our resolve, propelling us forward with unwavering determination.

As our mission expanded, we navigated challenges associated with growth. Like many African nations, Ethiopia boasts a rich tapestry of ethnic groups and languages. Yet, amidst this cultural diversity, intense conflicts fueled by political and religious differences frequently erupted, resulting in profound devastation and loss of life among tribal factions. Foreigners, particularly Westerners, were met with skepticism and often advised to avoid certain regions.

Aware of the risks posed to Westerners in remote Ethiopian areas, we proceeded cautiously, treading carefully and extending our reach only as far as safety allowed. We remained vigilant, attuned to the ever-changing dynamics on the ground, and mindful to avoid trouble while visiting new places.

We visited Shashemene, a busy city. Instead of donkey carts, the mode of transportation there was a little three-wheeled vehicle known as a *bajaj*. These little taxi carts moved people like mosquitoes and flooded the congested streets. Making our way through the crowds, we met with Abebe's contacts and toured the area, stopping at a vantage point that let us see most of the town, a place of dust and life, humming with untamed energy that seemed to pulse from the earth itself. Once lush and green, the rolling hills had been scorched by the relentless sun, leaving the landscape a patchwork of browns and golds. Despite the harshness of the terrain, the air was thick with the scent of spices, coffee, and hope. This strange, heady mixture reflected the resilience of the people who called this place home.

Small stalls lined the narrow roads, their wooden frames crooked but sturdy. People sold everything from fresh injera bread to vibrant fabric wraps fluttering like survival flags in the warm breeze. The town's rhythm was constant, a quiet thrum of daily life—footsteps on dry earth, distant laughter from children, the clang of metal pots and pans as vendors prepared for the day's trade. It was a town that bore its hardships openly, but beneath the surface was a pulse of determination, a will to push forward, no matter how unforgiving the conditions.

When I first arrived in Shashemene, the weight of its poverty pressed on me like the unrelenting heat, making me wonder if anything we did could be enough. But after seeing the programs take root in the red soil of other places, that weight shifted. Families who had once been on the brink of collapse were finding their footing. Small businesses—ones we had helped fund with micro-loans—were springing up in the markets, slowly transforming the face of other towns. Shashemene could do it too.

In Addis, a mother I'd met on our first trip was now running a thriving fabric stall, her colorful wraps catching women's eyes throughout the town. She had hired two other women to help her, creating a small network of support, a chain of survival that hadn't existed before.

A man who sold injera from a modest clay oven, bought with one of our first loans, now had a line of customers by mid-morning, their hunger lessened by his efforts. Their children, who once ran barefoot and dirty through the streets, were now clean, fed, and going to school.

I imagined the same successes elsewhere. As we talked with more people in Shashemene about what we could accomplish together, the air, once heavy with hopelessness, now carried something lighter, something brighter—hope. The transformation wasn't dramatic or sudden, but it was real. The small steps we took, discussing opportunities and planting seeds of sustainability, would grow.

The town still bore its scars, and the road ahead was long and uncertain. But in the quiet moments, when I walked through the town and saw the faces of those whose lives had changed with only the addition of hope, I knew we were on the right path.

When COVID-19 hit the world, we planned a trip back to Shashemene. Forced to cancel when the pandemic ramped up, we narrowly avoided violent conflicts in the city. Unrest following the assassination of Hachalu Hundessa, a prominent Oromo singer and activist, triggered widespread protests and violence across Ethiopia, particularly in the Oromia region, where Shashemene is located. In this turmoil, businesses, including the hotel we'd booked, were targeted in acts of politically motivated violence tied to broader ethnic tensions in the region. Terrorists burned the Haile Hotel, where we would have been, to the ground, leaving hotel guests fleeing in the middle of the night, barely escaping with their lives. Muslim extremists killed many people and burned down several Christian-owned businesses. Once more, it was as if God ensured we were safe, looking out for us, keeping us home.

Once we could travel again, we went to an area farther south and more remote than Shashemene, where the landscape transitions from the open plains of the Rift Valley to fertile farmlands and rolling hills. As you travel, you pass through Hawassa, a vibrant lakeside town known for its calm waters and bustling markets. Further south, Yirgalem offers lush coffee plantations and dense forests, a quieter town where the culture of coffee permeates daily life.

Continuing into the Sidama region, Wondo Genet is renowned for its hot springs and natural beauty, while Dilla, a busy market town, serves as a hub for the region's prosperous coffee trade. As you move deeper into the highlands, the terrain becomes more rugged and green, and coffee cultivation thrives in the volcanic soil of Gedeo and Guji. The southern route from Shashemene offered a glimpse into Ethiopia's diverse landscapes and rich cultural heritage, where rural life is deeply connected to the land.

Abebe said many people in this very remote area were beyond desperate. No other mission or humanitarian organization worked there at all. "People there aren't just poor; they are starving to death in what is known as ground zero for Muslim extremism in Ethiopia," Abebe said.

"Would we be safe?" I was wary of putting FHI staff in unnecessary danger after experiencing a few close calls myself. Plenty of people needed help who didn't want to kill us.

"Yes, and I believe we could make a real difference. The biggest worry is conflict between different tribes in the regions," Abebe told me as if that made it better. "If they killed us, it would probably be an accident."

"So, Muslim extremism and volatile cultural and political conflicts. No worries." My tone was wry, but my heart wondered what life was like for starving families without help or hope. It was hard to imagine people poorer and more helpless, living in worse conditions, even after all I'd seen.

Abebe was very familiar with the region. His brother-in-law, Pastor Zerihun, worked there, leading a team of missionaries who ministered to the poor. Hearing about Family Hope, Pastor Zerihun begged Abebe to help the women there.

"Most are single Muslim women with about ten children. In Muslim culture, men often have multiple wives and children, and many leave them to raise the children all alone," Abebe said as he led our team into the potentially hostile area known as Aje.

We picked up Pastor Zerihun along the way, in the middle of nowhere, who offered a wealth of information and guidance.

As we discussed the potential new project area and heard about the suffering of the families, I was still worried. Was it safe for our team to work for a Christian organization in a Muslim extremist area? The lepers of Korah had turned out to be kind and welcoming, but there was no guarantee we would receive the same warm welcome from the Muslims.

"Please, please, call me Z," Pastor Zerihun said. "Everybody does!"

Always smiling and laughing, he seemed carefree despite working in the most dangerous parts of the country. A tiny man, he's the biggest Ethiopian I know because of his giant faith and commitment, mile-wide smile, and contagious laugh. He was uncommonly easy and simple, and I admired him.

When I asked him about it, he shared, "I trust in God for my daily protection and provision."

"Z has the most amazing stories!" Abebe told us. "Stories that are hard to believe unless he tells them." He laughed. "So many times, his life has been in danger."

Again, I was not reassured and was full of questions for Pastor Zerihun as we approached the danger zone.

Pastor Zerihun told us harrowing stories about the many threats he'd faced and how close he had come to losing his life working in certain areas. What struck me most as he spoke was his bold, courageous faith and unwavering commitment.

I knew he had a family, and I wondered if he ever struggled with what his devotion could cost him. "Z, don't you realize you could be killed for your work in these areas?" I asked.

He burst out laughing, almost falling out of his chair. After recovering, Pastor Zerihun smiled. "Yes, I know I put myself in death's way."

"Doesn't that worry you?" Ethan asked.

"If they kill me, God will take care of my family. Why would I worry?" Pastor Zerihun said as if it was as simple as that. And, for him, it seemed to be.

Pastor Zerihun was the freest man I had ever met. Free because he gave his life to Jesus long ago and trusted Him to care for all of it. There was incredible simplicity to his faith. His was no shallow, circumstantial, or conditional faith. It was real and challenged me in new, unfamiliar ways. He made me ask about faith. How real was mine? How deep and how strong? Was it like a wood veneer covering the surface of my life, or was it like Pastor Zerihun's? Solid oak, hewn from the strength of genuine suffering, difficulties, and experience.

At lunch, at a tiny place in the middle of nowhere, Z told us about the time a group of men came to his house, planning to kill him. "They were on the road by my house, shouting my name when I walked up. There was no way I could escape them. Nothing I could do to run or hide."

"What did you do?" Pastor Randy, a team member from Boise, asked nervously, frowning.

"What I always do when I run out of options. I prayed for deliverance from these men and certain death. Then, I walked towards them. They stood still as if they had become blind and didn't see me, letting me pass and go safely home."

"That's incredible!" Pastor Randy exclaimed.

Pastor Zerihun nodded, his face round with a beaming smile. "Much better than when I started the church a few years before. The villagers assembled a mob to run me out and gathered at my home. They shouted, 'Come out! Come out! We want to kill you!' I had brought a new religion to them, and they wanted to kill me for it. All I could do was pray to God and ask Him to give me the courage to go out and face them. But their chants grew louder and angrier when I went to the fence. 'We are going to kill you!' they screamed. I shouted back, 'You can kill me, but I will live forever! Jesus is good for me, and He is good for you too!' At this, they went wild and ran in various directions, confused over my lack of fear and strange words." Z raised his arms over his head and burst into contagious laughter as he remembered his deliverance.

We finished our lunch of roasted goat and headed off the beaten path onto a rougher road. It was slow-going, navigating compact-car-sized potholes and endless donkey and ox carts. Everybody we passed stared intently at us, clearly wondering what in the world we were doing there.

In one small town, a large, well-dressed man stepped into the middle of the road and motioned for us to stop. He was wearing traditional Muslim dress—a turban and a long, white, robe-like garment tailored like a shirt but ankle-length and loose. His manner, clothing, and raised hand told me he was a leader.

We stopped the van a few feet from him. He stared at me, and I stared back from the passenger seat. *Here we go.* The strange man's imposing manner and the dangers I'd been warned about made my mind immediately go to ambush. Death. I should have reassured the team, but I watched along with them, heart in throat, as the van door slid open and Z walked toward the huge man, who looked even larger beside the diminutive pastor.

I thought we might end up in one of Pastor Zerihun's crazy stories until Z and the man grinned and embraced. The man clearly knew and liked Pastor Zerihun, which made him far less imposing.

"Well, I didn't see that coming." I laughed, letting out relieved energy and a whoosh of breath when Pastor Zerihun hopped back into the van, and we drove on.

Pastor Zerihun smiled wide, his eyes dancing. "That was the Muslim chief for this region. He runs the show here. Like a sheriff, what he says goes. But he knows us and the work we do. He knows I love his people and am here only to serve them."

"Z's being modest," Abebe said. "He works at forging relationships with everyone he meets. It took a while, but he got even that man to bless and allow him to pass through. Now, he's letting us in too. Different races. Different religions. We can all work together peacefully when we love and care for people who need it most."

We visited several desperate Muslim families in Aje. God loved them as much as he loved others, and we decided to launch FHI in the area if He opened the door despite the dangers.

Pastor Zerihun continued telling harrowing stories as we traveled farther south, keeping us glued to our seats.

"You don't hear stories like that every day in America!" Pastor Randy said after soaking in Pastor Zerihun's almost unbelievable tales for hours.

"Not too many years ago, Christians were heavily persecuted and killed in this region. Most were driven out. It was so bad that Muslims even burned a man's home down because he and other Christians were meeting there for prayer. He and his family barely escaped with their lives." Pastor Zerihun's eyes clouded at the memory.

"Z gathered the family together where the house had stood. In the smoking rubble, he led them in prayer. Fervently and loudly," Abebe said.

Pastor Zerihun shared what happened next. "Soon, a group of curious Muslim men gathered, listening to us pray. 'Oh, God, please forgive those who burned down this home. Please let them know we love and forgive them. Please let them come to know the love of Jesus,' we prayed. Eventually, the Muslims cried out, 'We burned your house down! Why would you pray for us? How could you forgive us?' I told them we forgave them as our Lord would, that He loved them just as he loved the family whose house they'd burned down. After that, something extraordinary happened."

"A miracle! That's what it was. A miracle," Abebe added.

Pastor Zerihun smiled and continued. "The men went away, and a brief time later, they returned with sticks and other materials to rebuild the man's home. Those who burned the house built a much nicer and larger home than before!"

"Since then, what began as a small gathering of five or six Christians grew to more than 800 with a large church recently built!" Abebe said.

"Do you think there's any way we could visit this place? Meet this man and see the church?" Pastor Randy asked, moved by the story.

"If it's not too much trouble to detour," I said. We had no plans to explore another area on our trip. "Abebe, would it be possible to take a portion of our team there?"

After a bit of discussion, Abebe said he could arrange it.

The next day, we headed off, arriving at the church in the afternoon after a typically rough ride that was otherwise uneventful.

The village of Hanicha was like many others we'd seen. It reminded me of Dembidolo with its remote beauty and desperately poor people. What sets Hanicha apart from other regions is its distinct cultural identity and traditions, which are deeply rooted in the local ethnic groups. The community practices unique music, dance, and festivals specific to the region, reflecting its rich heritage. The area is known for its agricultural lifestyle, with fertile land supporting crops like enset (false banana) and coffee, staples in the local economy. Hanicha's landscapes wow with vistas of scenic highlands and lush greenery, contributing to its unique natural beauty. The people rely on subsistence farming and livestock like sheep and goats for their livelihood. Hanicha is particularly isolated, with limited access to medical care and education. Many residents face significant challenges related to poverty and malnutrition.

Pastor Zerihun introduced us to the church leaders, who shared stories about their past lives as Muslims and how they'd become Christians, each tale more impactful than the last. "Hanicha has seen religious transformations, including the growth of a local Christian community, despite initial hostility," Abebe said.

"Still, despite all these good things, the church is impoverished. The people of Hanicha are the poorest I have ever seen," Pastor Zerihun told us sadly.

We visited many families so malnourished that they were on the very edge of life and death.

"These people need help, and they need it soon," Pastor Randy said, stricken by what he saw. "It's hard to reconcile such suffering in this part of Africa, where the potential is so clear, the land so potentially fruitful."

One of the pastors shared with us, "The drought has claimed many lives. There's no more food or clean water for those without funds or means to earn them. Death is the only escape for many people here." He handed Abebe a letter and said, "Could you read this letter I wrote to the government? If it seems right to you, please send it to anyone in the government you think could help when you return to the city."

Abebe read the letter as the pastor continued describing the dire situation in Hanicha. After a moment, Abebe smiled and passed the letter to Pastor Randy. "I believe this letter is meant for you. Earlier, you mentioned you weren't sure why you felt called to come to Ethiopia. It's as though this pastor wrote the letter to you and your church, and that God has led you here to be a partner through Family Hope, to help in ways the government never could," Abebe said. "Let this show you how God is using you to meet the needs of these people."

At that moment, the reason for our journey became clear—we were the answer to the Hanicha pastor's prayers and letters.

The timing and plea of the letter deeply affected Pastor Randy. "I knew I came here for a reason. Now, what can we do to help as fast as possible?"

Ethan said. "We just need to figure out logistics. Fast."

"God put all the right people and project pieces in place for us. We'll figure out the rest," I said, feeling none of the anxiety that once haunted me. I knew now that we could do it with God's help.

We spent the remainder of our visit exploring the area, witnessing firsthand the overwhelming poverty of the locals who followed us wherever we went. Much like in other regions, large crowds gathered around us whenever we stopped.

Despite initial concerns about potential Muslim extremism or hostility, we felt safe and welcomed. Shortly after that visit, with the invaluable support of our U.S. church partners, we launched project areas in Aje and Hanicha. These dedicated partners sponsored several families and accompanied us on subsequent vision trips to witness the impacts of our work firsthand.

Next, we visited Aje, nestled in the southern highlands of Ethiopia, where the earth meets the sky in sweeping, golden plains interrupted only by clusters of acacia trees and small, hidden rivers that wound their way through the landscape. The air there was dry but crisp, with the scent of wood smoke drifting from the simple mud and thatch homes that dotted the land. Life in these villages was woven deeply into the land itself, where the rhythm of the seasons determined the pace of daily life.

Homes were spread across the hills, their thatched roofs blending into the colors of the earth, creating the sense that the village had grown naturally from the land. Children played barefoot in the dust, their laughter rising in the air like the call of birds. The people, predominantly Muslim, moved with quiet grace, their simple lives marked by a deep sense of community and faith. Men tended to their small herds of cattle or worked the fields, while women wrapped in bright, handwoven shawls moved about the village, balancing water jars on their heads or kneeling to tend to their crops.

Hannicha, just beyond the hills, was smaller but equally resilient. The village lay along a narrow river that brought life to its arid surroundings. Here, women gathered at dawn, their chatter lively as they washed clothes in the cool, flowing water, their children playing nearby. The village was a hub of activity, with men working to build new structures out of mud bricks, their hands covered in the reddish soil that colored everything. At sunset, the call to prayer echoed softly across the valley, a reminder of the shared faith that tied the community together.

Aje and Hannicha were places of tradition where life moved slowly but purposefully. The people were proud and strong in their faith and connection to the land; though resources were scarce, their generosity knew no bounds. Visitors were welcomed with open arms, invited to share meals of injera and wat stew, and treated as family. The women, especially, were the heart of the villages—bold, resilient, and often the driving force behind the small markets and trade that kept the communities afloat.

What struck me most about Aje and Hannicha was their resilience. Despite their hardships—drought, poverty, isolation—there was a spirit here that could not be broken. Their lives were difficult, but their hearts were full, and in the quiet strength of the people, there was a profound beauty.

***

Upon our return, months after we had last walked the dusty roads of villages like Aje and Hannicha, we were greeted not only with warm embraces but with stories that defied expectation, stories of miraculous transformations, of families once on the edge of despair now standing strong, their lives forever changed. The risks we had taken, venturing into these forgotten, remote, and often perilous regions, felt justified. The profound impact on the communities we had touched was now more than just hope—it was reality.

Each project area presented challenges—sometimes more than we thought we could handle. The struggles were different in detail but identical in essence: the relentless need for food, clean water, education, and the simple dignity of providing for one's family. Yet, as we saw the tangible fruits of our efforts—the mothers now running small businesses, the children attending school with full bellies and bright eyes—it became clear that our work was more than charity. It was the start of something sustainable, something that could grow.

Encouraged by our progress, we became more committed than ever. Each success and every life we changed fueled a deeper resolve. We embraced the lessons we learned, refining our approach and becoming more effective and in tune with the rhythms of the communities we served. Throughout this journey, we remained grounded in the stories—those moments of joy and struggle that had become the heartbeat of our mission. The faces, laughter, and resilience of the people we served inspired us to expand our efforts and share our mission with others who might join us in carrying it forward.

In the following years, my journey took me to the farthest reaches of Ethiopia—places I had once only seen on maps, now etched into my memory with the faces and stories of the people who lived there. As I traveled those distant paths, I reflected on how far we had come, yet how much more there was still to do.

What awaited me on this path ahead? The question lingered like a quiet prayer, unanswered but full of promise. The road was uncertain, and the horizon stretched beyond what I could see. But I felt truly open—more open than ever to God's plan, ready to embrace whatever new horizon He laid before me.

Chapter Thirteen

Going Under, Fighting for Breath

As the FHI business and loan program found its footing and families blossomed with newfound independence, a sense of tranquility washed over me even as a profound revelation dawned, an awakening to the unyielding call of our mission. Beyond our achievements lay a vast expanse of need, a sea of souls awaiting salvation. The calm waters of accomplishment whispered a sobering truth—rest was a luxury we could not afford when God's work beckoned us onward, urging us to reach farther and deeper into the depths of human suffering.

I thought about the storms I'd weathered, the ways I stepped out in faith before sinking in fear, and the comfort zones that made me feel safe and secure, including my role leading Family Hope and our fantastic team. After many challenges, everything felt easy, more comfortable, and familiar. Leading wasn't as challenging and didn't require the same bold faith from me as before. I'd relaxed and stopped pushing myself as a leader in my faith. I needed to step out of my comfort zone again and inspire more people to join me.

The time had come to leave the safety of familiar shores and venture into uncharted waters. Family Hope stood poised to become a beacon of hope and transformation in the lives of those drowning in despair in other areas. I resolved to embrace boldness once more, to take daring risks, and to step forward in unwavering faith. Entire countries of drowning people cried out for salvation. How could I remain anchored in my comfort when the winds of opportunity beckoned us to hoist the sails of faith and navigate the depths of human need? The horizon awaited, alive with the promise of miracles yet to be realized.

"Lord, lead us into the unfamiliar, unknown, and uncomfortable so we can be a miracle to more families," I prayed.

At our January board meeting, I shared that God wanted us to expand into other countries. "The needs are great, but our God is greater, so let's prepare to navigate unchartered waters again," I said.

The leadership team embraced the expanded vision and contacted our mission and church partners about where we might partner outside Ethiopia. Eventually, we settled on Kenya and Kibera as our first targets. Kibera is one of the largest slums in all of Africa, with over one million inhabitants.

FHI leaders Abebe, Abonesh, Ethan, and I traveled there and explored the potential project area, spending time with our mission and church partners and meeting the critical leaders in Kibera.

Touring Kibera on foot, we found its size and conditions shocking. It was the most significant place of poverty we ever saw. Located in Nairobi, Kenya, life in Kibera is characterized by extreme poverty. Most residents live in overcrowded, makeshift houses made of mud, tin, and wood. Access to essential services such as clean water, sanitation, and electricity is minimal. Many households share communal toilets, often leading to unsanitary conditions contributing to health challenges like waterborne diseases.

The slum lacks formal infrastructure, and narrow, unpaved paths lead between densely packed homes. Open sewage flows through some of the streets, further exacerbating hygiene issues. Unemployment is high, and many residents survive on informal jobs such as small-scale trading or casual labor. Despite the hardships, Kibera has a vibrant community spirit, with local organizations and initiatives working to improve education, healthcare, and living conditions.

The area is also known for its complex social challenges, including crime and substance abuse. Still, it remains resilient with strong cultural bonds and grassroots efforts striving for positive change.

"The conditions in Kibera are awful. People crowd into tiny dwellings the size of an American bathroom. Dead animals and garbage are piled up everywhere. It looks like a war zone. So many people are in horrible physical condition due to disease and other illnesses. It's as bad as Korah and Dembidolo, if not worse, for no other reason than the much larger area and dense population with people crowded together, living on top of each other," our Kenyan country director, Kepha, told the group. He'd grown up in the Kibera slum. "I had eight siblings. We slept on the floor every night. There was never enough food, so the children would take turns deciding who could eat our one small meal each day. Daily life was a struggle with poverty."

Certain areas of Kibera were unsafe even with constant security. In other places, security advised us to stick together and keep moving, not to carry anything in our pockets, and to keep quiet. We complied to see the living conditions of the most impoverished people and families as we walked through winding streets and tiny corridors to poor families' small, dark living places.

We visited a man with advanced diabetes. The sadness and hopelessness in his eyes penetrated my soul. He showed us his used syringes and empty vials of insulin and said he had no money for more.

Without it, he would die. He pulled back a blue tarp, revealing his wife, who was nursing a baby. He was so ill from untreated diabetes that he couldn't work and take care of his little family anymore. Their situation was extreme.

"Working for tiny amounts of money when he can means they might only eat every few days," Abebe said.

I left the visit with this desperate man feeling more strongly than ever that our work was a matter of life and death. "How fast can we get here?" I asked Ethan.

Over the next few days, we visited many other impoverished families that needed our help as soon as possible. When we returned to the U.S., we worked diligently to launch the new project area only a few months later, one year after God's expanded vision. I asked our staff to make sure the man with diabetes and his family were one of the first families we sponsored, but sadly, he died not long after our visit.

My heart broke. "Help truly was a matter of life and death for him," I told Ethan. "The good news is that someone sponsored his wife and small child, and they're doing much better. We might have been too late to help that man, but his desperate plea saved his family and brought a river of hope to other desperate families in Kibera."

***

"Hey, Dad." I called him soon after I got home from my latest vision trip. After a few minutes of catching up, I said, "This might seem weird, but could we talk about when I was a kid and almost drowned up at Lake Minnetonka?"

"Sure. I remember. It was one of the scariest days of my life. What's going on?"

RIVER OF HOPE

"Everything's fine. I've been thinking a lot about that day lately, and I don't remember talking much about it as a kid. I'd love to hear how you remember it." I'd connected enough dots to know the trauma of my childhood drowning had stayed with me. I didn't know what my dad could add to fill in the blanks of my memory, but I wanted to know more.

"I can't speak for how it affected you, Son, but when I heard the splash of you going over and didn't see you, I didn't have time to think. I just ran to the front of the pontoon and jumped in. It was a leap in the dark. I didn't know how deep the water was, and there was no time to remove my glasses, wallet, or keys from my pockets. I just jumped in." Even all these years later, I heard the trauma of the moment as he relived that fateful day.

"You couldn't see anything in the water? Bubbles or anything?" I shivered, memories of the lake closing over me, tightening my throat.

"Nothing. The water was so murky and over my head when my feet touched the bottom of the lake. I waved my arms around, desperately reaching in the darkness, trying to find you, and racing against time. There was no sign of you. I was terrified! How much do you remember?"

I told him everything I recalled, finding it hard to breathe as memories flooded back and pressed down on me. "I always come back to memories of those terrifying moments when life gets overwhelming. The last thing I remember from that day is how the boat disappeared above me when the darkness swallowed me. I must have passed out."

"A lot almost changed that day," Dad said when I finished.

"I would have died if you hadn't rescued me. I wouldn't have grown up, married my high school sweetheart, looked into the eyes of my newborn baby girl, or experienced the joy of welcoming eleven children into our family. Or known our grandchildren," I said, seeing things in a way I hadn't before—the connections in all of it. I'd always looked at my life as a whole when the pieces were what mattered.

I'd experienced joys, sorrows, dreams, wins, losses, hurt, hope, and fear and would have missed them all had Dad not saved me. My parents would have grieved for the loss of their first-born son, burying me.

"I cannot imagine what it would have done to your mother," Dad said like he read my mind. "And the guilt would have eaten at me if you'd died on my watch. Who knows what would have happened to our marriage after such a terrible thing? Or to your brothers. They would have endured your death and our despair and would not have had all the times you shared growing up. Like dominos, they are, the lives a person touches in so many ways."

"It reminds me of *It's a Wonderful Life* when George realizes he'll never leave his hometown or explore the world and wishes he'd never been born."

"Until the angel shows him what life would've been like if he had never been here." Dad had seen the movie many times.

"Exactly. It would have been terrible for so many people. Do you remember what happens at the end?"

"The angel got his wings, and the townspeople, who loved George, saved the day," Dad answered.

I grinned. "Before that, though, Clarence jumped in the water and pretended he was drowning."

"That's right! He knew George would jump in to save him."

"He also knew that by jumping in to save someone else, George would ultimately be saved himself." My voice held the wonder of this revelation and others that followed in a rush.

"None of us can fully grasp how never being born would have affected the lives of those around us," Dad said. "Just like we can't know what life would have been like if you had died as a child that day at the lake, though I am so glad we will never find out."

My head swirled with newly connected thoughts and feelings when we hung up.

I've experienced the emotional equivalent of drowning, feeling paralyzed with fear, hopelessness, and desperation so many times. I thought of the dream I had about drowning babies and the man who jumped in to save them when no one else would. As a teenager and young adult, I was overwhelmed by anxiety and fear, and later, I struggled with worry and inadequacy over the mission's survival. Despite these challenges, I'd been saved from emotional drowning for a powerful reason, I realized, as the pieces of my life fit together in a way they never had before.

I talked with Chris about these revelations later that night. "I always thought of my rescue that day at the lake as a matter of life and death—my life and death. After talking with Dad and putting it in context with the rest of my life, I see that my living was a matter of life and death for many others. I see how drowning with fear and anxiety and a sense of lostness, so often overwhelmed and suffocating under the weight of responsibilities and fear of failure, I struggled in vain to save myself so many times when I just needed to turn to God for help."

"God was there with you all along. He jumped in to save you from drowning every time you finally cried out for His help," Chris said.

"You can't save a drowning man until he stops trying to save himself." I laughed and hugged her. "The way to salvation is surrender! It's about letting go of our efforts and trusting in God's plan and His ability to guide us through our challenges."

"People are drowning all around us, Jeff," Chris continued, her voice filled with compassion. "They might not show it on the outside, but they are desperate and in need. We can choose where to jump in and lend a hand as long as they never let go of their faith."

Her embrace was a comforting reassurance, a tangible reminder of the divine purpose that guided us on this remarkable journey, always with us.

"And I'll keep doing it," I affirmed, a profound sense of peace settling over me like a gentle wave. "God is opening doors in Africa and beyond. He wants His river of hope to flow wherever people are drowning in hopelessness and despair. It may be daunting, risky, or costly, but I'll jump in anyway because, for those who are drowning, it's a matter of life and death."

As night descended and the world grew quiet, I knew with unwavering certainty that this was only the beginning. With each new door opened by God's grace, I would continue to step forward, embracing the challenges and triumphs that lay ahead, driven by a deep-seated conviction that every life we touch, every orphan we prevent, and every family we set free, is a testament to the transformative power of faith and the boundless love of God.

Memories in Photos

Jeff and Ben, first trip

Entenesh and her daughter

JEFF BUTLER

Jeff and Ethan Bauer

Gutumuma women

RIVER OF HOPE

Judy and sponsored family, the day they met

Judy and sponsored family, one year later

JEFF BUTLER

Hanicha church

Pastor Z, Jeff, Abebe, and Wariso

RIVER OF HOPE

Jeff, Waganesh, and her son in Korah

Widow and orphan in orphanage

Make a Difference

People are dying because we're not acting. It's that simple. And deep down, we know it.

Most people won't step up to help unless they can truly see those in need as they see themselves: as precious human beings, just like us. But it's easy to look away when suffering is happening across the ocean. It's easy to ignore the faces we'll never see, the cries we'll never hear, and the problems we convince ourselves we can't solve.

People often ask me how Family Hope International does what we do. The answer is simple: we don't see orphans as someone else's problem. We see them as our own children. We see struggling mothers as our mothers and desperate fathers as our fathers. We embrace them as family, not because it's convenient, but because their lives are intertwined with ours in ways we can't ignore. We've heard their cries, seen their needs, and felt their pain—face to face. And in those moments, we realized they were more like us than we ever imagined.

We've witnessed firsthand the devastation of their countries—beautiful places ravaged by famine, drought, civil war, and indifference. And through it all, we've learned how much can be done with so little. What we take for granted, what we throw away without a second thought—could change entire families' lives.

When we heard their screams for help, we couldn't turn away. We drew closer, and we could hear nothing else once we did. The choice was clear: we could either watch people suffer and drown, or we could jump in and save as many as we could.

For most, it's hard to imagine the depth of suffering I've described. We don't often think that nearly one billion people, about 8% of the world's population, live on less than $3 a day. But this is the reality: while we live in abundance, billions struggle, starve, and die from circumstances we could change if we truly cared to act.

Here in America, we make up just 4% of the world's population, yet we control 25% of the world's resources. Think about that for a moment. The United Nations estimates that ending world hunger would cost between $30 and $160 billion a year—a number that seems impossible until you consider this: we spend nearly $5 billion yearly on snacks like Cheetos, Doritos, and Funyuns. We buy $3 billion worth of ice annually and throw away over $150 billion in food.

Imagine if we redirected just a fraction of that waste toward saving lives. That bag of chips you tossed could have fed a family. The money we spend on entertainment, dining out, or fireworks could be the difference between life and death for people across the world.

We have enough to feed the world's poor and end the poverty crisis. But global poverty isn't about a lack of resources. It's a failure to see those suffering as part of our human family. It's about failure to act.

As you read my story, I hope you see the bigger picture. We were all born for a purpose bigger than our fears, failures, or doubts. Yes, you have your own challenges, just like I did. But the fact that you are here, alive and reading this, means you have something important to offer. You have the power to save lives.

Maybe you've been sitting on the sidelines for too long, watching life pass you by, unsure how you can help. Maybe you feel too overwhelmed by your own struggles to think about helping others. But

I'm here to tell you that transformation begins by stepping out of your comfort zone. It's where miracles happen.

It's not too late. You can make a difference. You can change the world.

If you don't know where to start, I invite you to join us. There's room for you in this mission. Whether you want to sponsor a family, fund a small business, or become a partner in expanding our reach, we need you. Families are drowning in despair. We can help lift them out of it together.

Here are a few ways you can get involved:

- **Join a vision trip:** See firsthand the life-changing work we do and how you can make an impact.

- **Invite me to speak:** Whether at your church, business, or conference, I'd be honored to share our story and explore how we can work together.

- **Sponsor a family:** Your support will move a family through our process of embracing, equipping, empowering, and employing them, leading to long-term self-sustainability.

- **Fund a small business:** Give families the tools to break free from poverty and build a brighter future.

- **Become a vision partner:** Support the long-term vision of Family Hope International by helping us underwrite our operational costs and expand into more countries to serve more families.

You don't have to do it all, but you can do something. Together, we can create lasting change, one family at a time.

RIVER OF HOPE

Visit us to learn more and take the first step.

Family Hope INTERNATIONAL
Freeing Families from Extreme Poverty

Website

www.familyhopeinternational.org

Instagram

www.instagram.com/familyhopeinternational/

Facebook

www.facebook.com/familyhopeinternational

YouTube

www.youtube.com/@familyhopeinternational

Note from Jeff

Since my first trip to Ethiopia, I've encountered my fair share of challenges. It hasn't been an easy road, filled with uncertainties and unexpected twists. Yet, like navigating turbulent waters, every step of this journey holds profound meaning as it leads us into uncharted territories and new countries.

We remain steadfast in following wherever God's calling takes us, much like a river flowing toward the sea, guided by unseen currents. Despite the ongoing challenges that come with our work, we press forward because we believe deeply in the intrinsic worth of every person we encounter. The struggle is real, but knowing that we are making waves of positive change in people's lives makes it all worthwhile.

When I have doubts, I ask myself what would have happened if we stayed home, played it safe, and sat in the boat. Where would the diabetic man's family be today? Would they be alive? What about Etenesh? How long could she have fought off the hyenas at her door before her strength failed? How about those two little children who would have been abandoned on the streets by their mother if we hadn't shown up with Judy, who jumped in to save them? What would have become of all those other families we helped survive?

In the years since my adventures began, I have undergone a profound transformation, learning to trust God more. With His help, I overcame obstacles, fears, and insecurities and became stronger and more resilient. Once seemingly disconnected, I saw so many puzzle pieces of my life become a cohesive and scenic picture. My past experiences, good and bad, have uniquely prepared me for my life calling.

I am incredibly grateful for the amazing people God called to jump in and swim upstream with me to reach more families. I continually thank God for His guidance and provision and for using others to challenge me when needed. Their support and your interest in my journey are deeply appreciated.

I am deeply grateful for my beautiful wife, Crystal, who has always been there with wise words, encouragement, and love. She's the world's greatest mother and an incredible behind-the-scenes leader. Tough, with a big heart, she is loving, giving, selfless, solid, and straightforward. We took this journey together; without her support, there would be no Family Hope International.

Thanks, Dad, for jumping into that lake to save me (that was a good decision!) and for all the ways you and Mom have been there throughout my life.

I am deeply thankful for my buddy Ethan, whose friendship and leadership I cherish. Serving with him has been a great blessing and joy. FHI would never have made it without his capable leadership and big heart. We make an incredible team. Our close friendship is part of the mission's secret sauce.

For Ben, whom God used in many significant ways in my life. Thank you for inviting me on that first trip to Ethiopia. It's all your fault! And I love you for it.

For Michele Budka at Full Sail Publishing. Without your guidance, partnership, and expertise, I could not have authored this book. I am so thankful we took this journey together.

Family Hope International would not exist without the incredible leadership of my dear friends Abebe and Abonesh, who played vital roles in its development.

I'm thankful for Morgan, Jessica, Sarah, Kepha, Joy, and all our extraordinary U.S. and international leadership and staff. Their commitment and faithfulness to our sponsors and sponsored families make this work.

Finally, a huge thank you to our supporters, sponsors, vision partners, and church partners. You are the reason we can do what we do.

As I continue to navigate life's unpredictable currents, I am reminded that just as my dad saved me from drowning, God extends His hand of grace to lift us when we feel overwhelmed. His love is the anchor that steadies us amidst the storm, and His light is the beacon that leads us safely through the darkness. May you find solace and strength in the certainty of His presence, guiding us with unwavering love toward the shores of redemption and peace.

Reflecting on this journey filled with unexpected turns, impossible challenges, and miraculous moments, I am reminded of one truth: none of it was ever about me. From the early days of following a whisper in my heart to standing in the middle of a leper village in Ethiopia, I was never the one in control. God was the author of this story, and I was simply a vessel for His plans.

The brokenness I encountered in those distant places shook me to my core, but the hope that emerged from that brokenness changed me—and countless others—forever. What began with a simple desire to make a difference became a mission far greater than I could have imagined, one that continues to grow and evolve, driven by the power of faith, love, and community.

Through it all, I've learned that God's vision for our lives is always bigger than we dare to dream. He doesn't call us to be comfortable or certain—He calls us to be faithful—to say yes when it's hard, to step into the unknown when the path ahead seems impossible, and to love when it demands sacrifice.

To those reading this, I want you to know the story is not over. It's still unfolding. Children are waiting, families are on the edge of despair, and communities are desperate for hope. There is so much more to be done. And this isn't just my journey. It's a journey we can all be a part of. Whether through your prayers, your support, or your own steps into service, the invitation is here. You don't have to travel across the world to make a difference, but you do have to open your heart.

I pray that you'll join us, that you'll see beauty in saying yes to the call, and that together, we can continue to lift families from despair, rebuild lives, and bring light to the world's darkest corners.

Because in the end, it's not about what we achieve—it's about the lives we touch, the hope we spread, and the love we share. And that is a legacy worth leaving.

Meet Some Graduates

Some people we sponsor are so fearful and scared about taking out loans or paying them back. It's amazing watching them do it anyway. They come in so hopelessly. They can't even imagine feeding their kids or running a business. Most are initially overwhelmed and think they can't do it, but they sign up anyway, desperate to feed their kids. It's an emotional ride for the moms.

Every day, I see the ripple effect of how our families inspire others to think of solutions they never thought of before, like the woman in one community who started selling soap and organized her friends into a group that got land from the government and opened a community shower house.

The beauty of the people we work with, the joy and light in the kids' eyes, their smiles, and their parents' incredible strength in trying new things will always amaze me.

Here are a few of the stories of our graduates in their own words:

My name is Abebech. When I tried to find a job, no one would hire me because I had no education or experience. My son and I were alone in an empty house with almost nothing to eat. I used to stress a lot about how I was going to get our next meal and whether I'd be able to send my son to school. I used to come to the church and cry and beg the Lord to answer my prayers and ease my pain. Then, a miracle happened, and I joined this organization. I started getting monthly donations at first, and I had some money to put food on the table. After that, I was offered a loan so I could work and stand on my own feet.

After I took the loan, I started to sell clothing on the street. This experience has helped me financially and psychologically, relieving me from tremendous stress. Now me and my son live happily. He is attending school properly and always goes with a full-packed lunch. He graduated from kindergarten, and that made me even happier. Besides fulfilling my family's basic needs, I have been saving for the future. I'm forever grateful. Your help has been invaluable for my family. May God bless you.

My name is Marta Likasa. I have three daughters, and my husband died. When my husband died, Family Hope International started supporting my family. I have been leading my life by working as a daily laborer, and I earn twenty-five birr per day (less than 50 cents USD). My life before you started supporting me was full of troubles. I did not have anything to feed my children and could not cook food for my children at home since there was nothing to cook. I bought baked injera at the market to feed my children. But one day, God came to change my family's life through FHI. God has reached us at the end. The neighboring people do not know me, and nobody cared about my family. After FHI started supporting my family, I have seen a bright thing in my future.

I can cook for my children, and they are able to attend school. My sponsors have bought me a bed and bedding as extra support. I have not needed to buy any additional food. One of my daughters has graduated from Wollega University, and the second one will graduate this year. My third daughter got married, and she has started leading her life. Concerning my microloan, I had never had that much money before. The loan has helped me in many ways, and my life has changed because of it. I could not afford clean water, but now I can. I have a place in the market where I can sell coffee and other produce from my property. I have made a profit, and it helped me build my house. I have cash in my account and a small farm with seeds and fertilizer. I would like to bless FHI sponsors and the staff for what they have done for my family and me. May God bless you and your families abundantly.

My name is Bushu Moroda. My life before Family Hope International started supporting me is very different from that of today. My children were scattered due to poverty. It was very difficult. At that time, I was working as a daily laborer, making maybe ten birr (less than twenty cents USD) per day if I got that work. If not, I went to sleep without eating at night. FHI has supported my family for the last eight years, and their support is monthly. After they started supporting my family, I have seen a bright future. We received food to eat, and I have started preparing meals for my children as a woman does. My children have returned to school; they got exercise books, bags, and school uniforms. They have been distributing us teff, maize, oil, soap, peas, exercise books, bags, and pens; we have been getting food support every month. My sponsors have even bought me a bed, bedding, and clothing. They have fixed my roof so now I am living in a good house. Since FHI has started supporting my family, I have not bought any additional food from the market. Monthly distribution was enough for my family. I have repaid my loan. I have been working in the market, and from that loan profit, I have bought housing materials, shoes, and some things for my daughter. I have also supported my scattered children where they are. I have farmed a small plot of land with some people and shared the product. Finally, I would like to bless the supporting families for what they have been doing for me and for poor people like me. May God help you forever and ever. May God remove any obstacles in front of you and your families.

My name is Nigatu Tesfaye. Before Family Hope International started supporting my family, I was leading my family life by washing clothes for others. I also was collecting coffee beans as a daily laborer. Since I did not have anything to feed my family, I had to work every day, so I did not get a chance to worship God with my church members. Nevertheless, after FHI started supporting my family, I got everything I needed for my children and I now had time to worship God, as well as serve the church. I was able to stop working as a daily laborer when I received the microloan. It was amazing to start receiving support from FHI. From that day onwards, my family life started moving upward. Thanks to almighty God, we have been getting food support every month, and I have not had to purchase any food. I am working in my business and selling injera. My eldest son was able to get a driver's license thanks to my profit. I have saved money and been able to purchase things for my family. I would like to bless God and my sponsor families for the great things God has done through them. This is amazing for me and for people like me. I will start supporting people who need support as much as God allows me to do so.

My name is Argene Lamu. Our life before FHI started supporting us was very difficult. At that time, we did not have anything to eat. Not even teff was in my house. We ate sorghum with maize. But after FHI started supporting me, my family's life has changed, and we have seen a bright future. My family receives teff, maize, soap, oil, sugar, and peas and has also been gifted a bed, bedding, clothing, and many other things. I received a microloan, and this money has done so much for me. I was able to purchase sheep as well as two plots of land with coffee plants on them. I share the product equally with the owner of the coffee plant. I have purchased good seeds as well as fertilizer to help farm the land with my family. When the coffee and maize are harvested, I will make over $1,700. I am completely independent now and have money in my savings account. I would like to bless Family Hope International sponsors as well as all the staff for what they have done for my family.

My name is Zebeda Gambel. My life was so difficult before you started supporting my family. Before you started supporting me, I did not have food in my house or goods to prepare it. I would buy injera from the market and feed that to my family. Once FHI started helping my family, I was able to prepare food for the first time thanks to the support of teff, maize, oil, soap, peas, etc. We received food support every month, and I have not had to buy additional food at the market. I started selling vegetables in the market upon receiving the microloan. I was able to purchase a bed and bedding with the profit. I have savings of about 15,000 ETB (over $260) as well as some cash in my hand to use for my business or as needed. I am now independent. I do not need any more support from any organization. I would like to bless FHI and my sponsors for what you have done for me and for my family. May God add years to your lifetime. May God open new ways to you and your families. May God give you health since you have helped me in all things.

For more graduate stories, pictures, and videos, please visit our website www.familyhopeinternational.org. While you're there, drop me a line to get involved.

About the Author

Jeff Butler and his wife Crystal are devoted parents to eleven children. Jeff's journey, intricately woven with the blessings of God and adoption spanning the United States, Ethiopia, and China, ignited a passion for preventing orphans and empowering families, reflecting his deep commitment to making a difference. Now, he inspires others to join his mission, transforming lives and breaking the cycle of extreme poverty one family at a time.

Made in the USA
Columbia, SC
01 May 2025